Headline

MEMOIR OF A MEDIA CEO

D. D. PURKAYASTHA

Copyright © D. D. Purkayastha 2024
All Rights Reserved.

ISBN 979-8-89277-829-9

This book has been published with all efforts taken to make the material error-free after the consent of the author. However, the author and the publisher do not assume and hereby disclaim any liability to any party for any loss, damage, or disruption caused by errors or omissions, whether such errors or omissions result from negligence, accident, or any other cause.

While every effort has been made to avoid any mistake or omission, this publication is being sold on the condition and understanding that neither the author nor the publishers or printers would be liable in any manner to any person by reason of any mistake or omission in this publication or for any action taken or omitted to be taken or advice rendered or accepted on the basis of this work. For any defect in printing or binding the publishers will be liable only to replace the defective copy by another copy of this work then available.

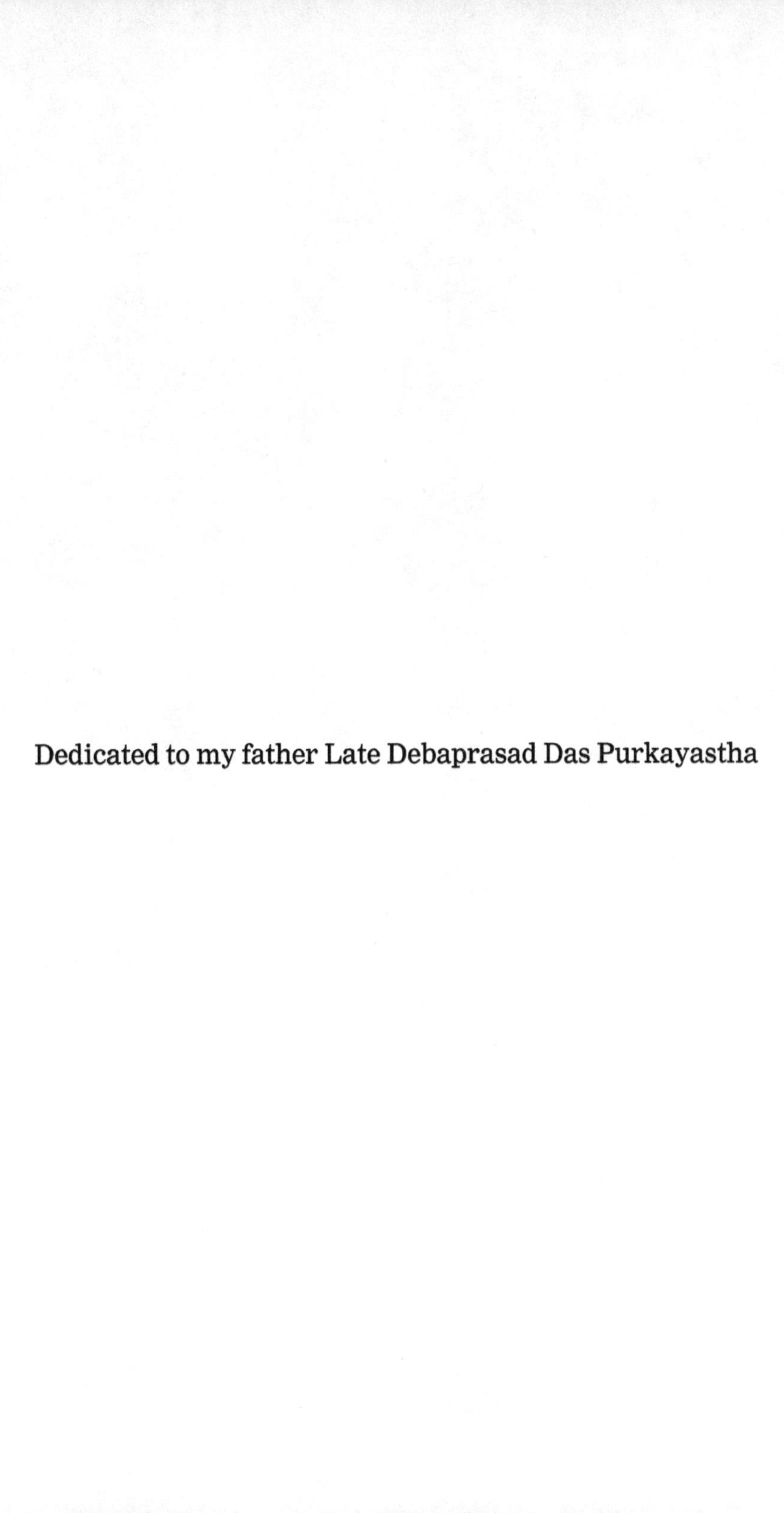

Dedicated to my father Late Debaprasad Das Purkayastha

Contents

An engaging story from a top media industry CEO. A truly unique & detailed insight into navigating a long career & the people who contributed to it (in both work & at home). It's a lesson for all: the twists & turns, the ups & downs, the challenges & successes. It even ends with his fifteen top tips for life (covering both business & personal life), which I personally will be taking onboard.

– Mark Challinor
CEO, News Media UK and former global President, INMA.

This book is 50 years of experience and wisdom distilled into 140 pages told in the form of DDP's own personal and professional journey. It is also a perspective on Indian media's journey in which DDP and ABP were important players and DDP had a ringside view. He tells it in his trademark sincere, thoughtful, and humble way. Thoroughly enjoyable and engaging, and a must read for everyone interested in understanding the evolution of Indian media with a hearty serving of "life lessons" from an outstanding media CEO and human-being.

– Deepak Goyal
Managing Director and Senior Partner, BCG, New York

This is a wonderful book by a brilliant man in a brilliant media group. Honest and unpretentious, it is a story well told. An enriching, energising read.

– Jacob Mathew
Managing Editor
Malayala Manorama & Past President, WAN-IFRA

I have had the privilege of knowing D.D. Purkayastha for over a decade, since he joined the INMA Board during my tenure as President. D.D. was instrumental in leveraging his extensive experience as a media CEO in India, significantly enriching our mission with his insights and dedication towards enhancing the global news media landscape. More than a valued colleague, D.D. has been a friend whose integrity and visionary leadership I deeply admire.

– Yasmin Namini

Digital Media Consultant and Advisor/Former Chief Consumer Officer, The New York Times/Past President, International News Media Association (INMA)

Headline is the compelling story of D. D. Purkayastha : of how he rose from humble beginnings and went on to become the CEO of ABP Group. He played an important role in shaping its future and the media landscape in India. He led the entry of ABP Group beyond newspapers into television and digital media. He elevated ABP on to the global stage at International forums such as WAN-IFRA and INMA. Included in the book are a set of life lessons which can help any young executive.

– Ranjit Pandit

Ranjit Pandit was a Director (Senior Partner) at McKinsey & Company who established the India practice in 1993. After completing a career spanning 27 years he went on to lead the investment activities of General Atlantic in India between 2007-2012. Today he runs his own businesses and serves on a variety of leading Boards

"I have known DD through our mutual advocacy for the essential role that journalism and news media plays in our community. We both served together on the board of the International News Media Association; DD for 8 years, and a decade for my part. During that time, I have come to know DD as a leader who exudes equal parts of purpose, professionalism, passion and indeed, persistence. In reading his memoir, his purpose is revealed readily, and he seeks to generously inspire the next generation of leaders to do better than those who have come before."

– Damian Eales

Damian Eales is the CEO of Move Inc, operator of Realtor.com, America's first and most trusted digital real estate portal. Move Inc is owned by News Corp where Damian has been a senior executive for over a decade.

Prologue

"To work, to work, such an infinite delight!"

– Katherine Mansfield

All lives are journeys, all of them unique in their own fashion. This is the telling of mine. I wouldn't be telling it if I did not think it is worth.

Every examined life has a central strain to it, like a vertebral column that marks out a path, holds everything together, and lends it curvature, this way and that. It could be anything and it will reveal itself upon, as I said, examination. It could be anything—an idea, a theme, a way of looking at the world around you, a way of interacting, or a way of responding. Anton Chekhov, master of the short story, would famously run away from situations, situations that he found difficult to come to grips with. And in so running away, he perfected what was central to his being: writing.

I often look back and wonder what it is that may have been central to my being and what it made of me, and I would say two things—a constant sense of revelling in what I did and the pursuit of how I could do that even better. I must consider myself very fortunate I spent the essential years of my life, especially my professional life, enjoying what I did, even when the going got tough.

The purpose of writing this book is primarily to bring some understanding and perspective to the workings of the media industry, arguably one of the most formidable levers of the modern world, the one factor central to all human engagement and endeavour—whether it is geopolitics and power, or the economy and industry, science and its ever-exploding frontiers from climate change to the critical exploration of mankind's past, it is media that has become the key dynamism of our times. Information, as has been famously suggested, is ammunition. Media is no longer about relaying or broadcasting events; it has verily become the agency of much of what happens around us. It is possessed of a scope and speed that is breathless.

In the Indian context too, the zooming outreach and influence of the media, and its ability to intervene in critical aspects of our daily lives, can barely be exaggerated, especially now when electronic and social media platforms have transcended the literacy barrier— news, or information, has ceased to be the preserve of those who can read and write. In a country like ours, where literacy remains relatively deficient, the exponential consumption of information driven by technology is nothing less than revolutionary. It is an exciting world but no less a challenging one.

Everyone is familiar with the glitz and glamour associated with media. But very little is known about the backend, the real engine-rooms that fuel the enterprise that we call by the omnibus term media. I would venture that what transpires behind the scenes, and which few get a view of, is far more exhilarating than the exterior. After spending more than four decades in one of the leading media companies in India, the venerable Ananda Bazar Patrika, or ABP, I thought it would be apt, indeed useful and instructive, to leave behind a narrative that may cast some light on the complex mechanics of the media industry.

I recently retired as Managing Director and CEO of ABP and began to sense soon after that I must put to paper a record of my journey, personal as well as professional—part memoir, part a manual of media management. To be honest, I must also state that the writing of this book has also been a function—a pleasurable function—of soaking up some of the free time I suddenly seem to have come into upon my retirement.

It is a matter of no mean delight and fulfilment to me that the writing of this volume coincided with the run-up to the centenary of *Anandabazar Patrika*, the Bengali daily that is also the mothership of the ABP enterprise. *Anandabazar Patrika* was launched in 1922 as a voice of protest against colonial rule. Mohandas Karamchand Gandhi had returned from South Africa just a few years ago and begun his journey towards becoming Mahatma, or Bapu. The draconian Rowlatt Act had recently been passed; one of the consequences of opposing it was the enactment of the horrifying massacre of Jallianwala Bagh. It had left the nation numbed and angered. Rabindranath Tagore forsook his Knighthood in protest and in 1921, the first non-cooperation movement was launched. The nation was in ferment. Anti-imperialist sentiment was surging all across. It was in the crucible of such tumult and nationalist fervour that *Anandabazar Patrika* was born. Symbolic of what it stood for, it was printed in red ink. The tradition of telling the truth fearlessly remains our leitmotif to this day. *Anandabazar*, as it has come to be known, played a significant and leading role in influencing the social, cultural, economic and political history of Bengal. It is no exaggeration to say that *Anandabazar Patrika* has been, and remains, the central listening post of Bengali lives and times. It has touched every Bengali mind and soul across the globe. It is so emotionally connected to its readers that their mornings do not proceed without having read the paper.

I am aware that what you are about to read is a jagged tale, moving back and forth in memory and in time. But that is how, to my mind, it is best told, for that is how the tale came to me as I sat down to write. I leave it to you, dear reader, to pick from it what you will. As the German scholar-philosopher, F. Max Muller wrote in his acclaimed work on the sage Ramakrishna Paramahansa: "Although in a grain of paddy, the germ is considered the only necessary thing...while the husk or chaff is considered to be of no importance... To get a crop, one must need to sow the grain with the husk on..."

Foreword by Dr Ashok Ganguly

I first met the author in Kolkata at the office of *Anandabazar Patrika*, the famous Bengali daily newspaper, a must-read among Bengalis across the world.

I personally knew virtually nothing about India's family-owned and 'managed' businesses, although these represented the bulk of India's private sector industry history. I was persuaded to join ABP in a non-executive role. Two family members, Aveek Sarkar, the then Editor-in-Chief, and his younger brother, Arup Kumar Sarkar, the expert who knew everything there is to know regarding the heart and soul of the news business. ABP's English newspaper, *The Telegraph*, was launched in 1982. The venerable weekly Desh was my late mother's favourite, as well as a few other well-known weeklies and periodicals. Soon after, I got to meet the CEO, Mrs Shobha Subrahmanyan, and the author, the then CFO. They were a formidable but silent team of rare operators of deep commitment, competency, and professionalism, comparable and maybe even better in some sense compared to those I have known.

During the ABP Board meetings, I had a deep commitment to at least partly professionalise some of the operations of the company. During these meetings, while the author was the best informed, he was also the quietest of those attending, with all the commercial data at the tip of his memory. This was at a time when McKinsey had done one of their 'polishing shoes to bible reading' analyses of the business, and CEO Shobha Subrahmanyan was leading the rejuvenation of this venerable organisation. For personal reasons, Shobha, a quietly spoken but outstanding leader, had to permanently move back to her home city of Bangalore. She was replaced by a reputed professional, recruited freshly to ABP. This change did not work out, and soon, the author was appointed to the role.

This is the subject of this book - Memoirs of a Media CEO, which captures his riveting account of not only what the media business is all about but a more profound narrative of how individuals in India emerge from the obscurity of back and beyond nooks and crannies of our vast country to rise into professional prominence, by their professional leadership and contribution to modern business and trade.

To my great satisfaction and surprise, although I had spent my career in a multinational organisation, I had the pleasure of meeting and admiring the professional success of the author in a privately held media business while achieving prominence in related activities internationally.

Family-owned businesses in India are known to value and reward the performance of their professional employees, but I do not know of many like ABP, which enabled the author to blossom professionally in India and abroad. ABP has grown into a rising star in the speedily changing Indian media horizon, gaining prominence across the expanding vernacular language channels while exploring emerging IT-driven opportunities and beyond.

The author's book has done a tremendous service by describing the cooperative advantages of global media associations while cooperating without sacrificing the competitive spirit.

The narrative of the transformation of the author's family and personal life echoes the transformation of the lives of middle-class professionals in India, a narrative that has been growing relentlessly as value creators and corporate leaders.

Dr Ashok S Ganguly was the Chairman of Hindustan Lever Ltd from 1980 to 1990 and a member of the Unilever Board from 1990 to 1997. Dr Ganguly has held board level positions with various other multinationals, including Hindustan Lever, ICI India, British Airways, Wipro, Tata AIG Life Insurance Co, Hemogenomics, and Firstsource Solutions. He was a member of the board of British Airways Plc from 1996 to 2005.

He was awarded Padma Bhushan in 1987, CBE in 2006 and Padma Vibhushan in 2009.

1

Beginnings

"It matters not where you come from, it matters where you go."

– Ernest Hemingway

I believe in a slight variation of what the great novelist and Nobel laureate said — I think both things matter: where you come from and where you go.

I am one of Midnight's Children, born in the year that our country came to freedom: 1947. The original roots of my family lie in the depths of Sylhet, which went to East Pakistan upon Partition and was lost in a haze no longer easy to access.

If I were to call somewhere home, it would be Hailakandi in Assam. Try to locate it on a map, and you will find that from our part of Bengal, you must traipse across the breadth of Bangladesh to reach it. Hailakandi lies at the confluence of multiple regions and cultures: bounded by Bangladesh to its west and the north-eastern states of Mizoram, Manipur and Meghalaya to the South, East and North.

The place of my birth, though, is farther up to the north in Assam, in the town of Digboi. My maternal uncle and aunt were both doctors based in Digboi at the time. It was my aunt, who headed the maternity hospital, who delivered me to the world. Decades later, on my 60th anniversary, I travelled back to the hospital with my wife, children, and grandchildren; it was like a pilgrimage of sorts to the place of my earthly origin. Digboi is a refinery town, and by then, the hospital has come under the auspices of the Indian Oil Corporation. We were shown around the premises by the staff — they knew in advance of our visit, so they had arranged a heartwarming welcome rite, complete with garlands and whatnot. One of the senior staff then dusted out a huge register from the record rooms and rolled its pages back to the birth entries of October 16, 1947. And there it was, for all of us to see: the first notings of my presence on this planet. It was from these records that I would learn, for the first time, that my birth was actually a complicated one; the umbilical cord had gotten coiled around my neck during the delivery, and for just a little while, I was in a state of strangulation. It was the deft hands of my aunt that got me breathing, probably wailing, too, as most newborns are meant to do.

Peering into the register of my birth was one of those moments one does not easily forget. My wife — and we shall soon come to her — was so overcome by emotion that she announced then and there that she wished to make a donation to the hospital: Rs twenty lakhs, she said. Such is the bureaucracy that surrounds even the simple act of a donation in our public sector enterprises that her wish to redeem the pledge of donation still lies caught up in red tape. I shall have to wait to complete that tale another time.

* * *

Hailakandi was where my childhood memories are from; it's where I went to school and spent my formative years. In many ways, that was the time that made me who I am.

My mother used to teach at the local school for girls. My father was a teacher too, but he was more than just that; he was a man of many splendorous parts. He taught English at the only college in Hailakandi, but he had also been a bank manager, he had studied and practised law; for a while, he was also a journalist. He worked on a retainership with the Amrita Bazar Patrika and would often be sending off reports from various parts of Assam that he was familiar with and would visit from time to time.

My father had ambitions for me; he wanted me to make something of myself. He was an idealist and a dreamer. He was also a man of deep knowledge. He was constantly engaged in the process of passing on his values and beliefs to me. He explained to me the scriptures of the Gita and the Upanishads. He inculcated in me a belief in the Almighty. He opened to me his beloved and treasured chest of English and Sanskrit literature. It seemed to me he had made it a mission of moulding me to a fineness. Probably with this in mind, he sent me off for a while to study in Agartala, a bigger town with better colleges. I stayed there with my uncle's family and did my higher secondary at MBB College, the best college in Agartala. The ambition, though, fed into me constantly by my father, was always to go to Calcutta and make a life in the big city. I had harboured this ambition in my heart since my early teens.

I did very well at school; I don't recall exactly, but I was the topper in the higher secondary examination under Calcutta University from the state of Tripura. That performance was to become my launchpad to Calcutta.

The year was 1962, I was barely fifteen, and I had my father's blessings to go explore the world. My father told me St. Xavier's College in Calcutta was the best institution for studies. My dream was to graduate with honours in Physics. In fact, Presidency College, one of the most renowned colleges in India, offered me admission with honours in Chemistry, which I refused. I had more than qualifying grades for entry to St. Xavier's. But there was a problem. I arrived at St. Xavier's a month after the admission process had closed; I had no idea. I met the then Vice Principal Fr. J. de Bonhome, a Belgian Jesuit with a stiff upper lip. To him, it was either yes or no and nothing in between. He told me that I was late and that classes started a month ago. Although my academic record was excellent, he couldn't admit me. I decided what I had to do then and there. For the next ten days, I sat on Fr. Bonhome's stool outside his room from nine in the morning until five. Every time he would emerge, I would ask him about my admission, and every time he would respond with a firm no, he would shrug and say sorry, you arrived late. But finally, one day, he yielded. When he said that I wouldn't be able to catch up with the class, I threw a challenge of sorts, telling him that if I did not make the first ten in class in the next examination, I would quit my studies. He had no answer. Thus, I started my B.Sc. course in Physics. He was pleased no end when I stood second in the exams. I remember he wrote a letter to my father praising the perseverance of his son; my father must have felt rather proud. To begin with, I stayed with another uncle in New Alipore but soon got a berth in the Hindu Hostel. I wanted to go to IIT, Kharagpur, for further studies — a proper B.Tech. specialising in electronics and telecommunications — and I even passed the entrance. But my family, keen as they were to see me do better and fulfil my ambitions, never had the financial resources to afford to send me to IIT. I had to decline the admission; I settled for a B. Tech course in Applied Physics at the more moderate — and affordable — Rajabazar Science College in Calcutta.

Calcutta in the sixties was the most happening city in India. Every industry except pharma and textiles was headquartered in Calcutta. Every global airline touched the city. It was one of the country's most sought-after centres for education and healthcare. The second jewel in the former British Empire had retained its glory and brilliance in full. Opportunities were booming. I used to dream about making it to the top management cadres of some big corporate house. I was topping my class. Everything seemed rosy.

But in 1964, my father was diagnosed with Angina Pectoris. Bypass surgery or angioplasty was unknown in those days. Medicines could extend his life but not beyond a decade or so, specialists said. My father was forced to go on long leave without pay. That's when I had to bury my IIT dreams.

I started applying for jobs in order to sustain the family. I got an offer from the renowned manufacturing firm GKW, which had a factory in Howrah. It was a costing and accountancy job — not the kind of start I had imagined after studying Applied Physics — but I did not have a choice nor the luxury to hesitate. I knew neither costing nor accountancy; I merely used common sense to secure entry. During the job interview, I was asked how I would calculate the unit cost of one pencil from a total of a thousand. I knew no formula I could apply, so I simply said I would calculate the total cost of wood and carbon required, add the labour and production costs, and divide it by a thousand. The gentleman interviewing me immediately asked his junior to give me the job.

I knew my life had radically changed its trajectory, but I took the change in my stride and forged on. Looking back, I often sense that destiny had plans for me. At that time, it seemed like I was being shuffled about helplessly by my circumstances — doing a cost accountant's job in a noisy manufacturing plant after securing a first class in Physics from the best-known college in Calcutta. But it was all part of an elaborate jigsaw whose pieces were being put together by destiny, quite unbeknownst to me.

It made my ailing father very sad to learn I had taken up an accountant's job; he knew I was a bright science student, and he had bigger dreams for me. But he, like me, also realised that there was a family to run and money to be earned to run it. Having graduated in Physics with flying colours, I now had to become a qualified accountant, too. It was hard going. I would work at the GKW facility in Howrah all day, then come home and study accountancy. I had to be self-taught through postal instruction, but I was a stubborn young man. I persisted. I burnt the proverbial midnight oil studying accountancy, which I held up with a day job to keep the family provided for. All of these labours would coalesce one day to make me a fuller, multi-faceted professional, although I did not entirely grasp it at that time.

* * *

It was also such a time in my life that I met a girl called Kamala. She would become my wife and the axis around which the whole family would hold itself together.

Kamala was studying to graduate in literature and history when I met her. It was love at first sight. I found in her a woman of strong will and confidence. She wrote poems, and often, her letters to me were her poems. We courted for six years before we decided to get married.

But it did not come easy. My parents didn't approve of my marrying a girl who was not from our community and geography. Kamala wouldn't have agreed to marry without my parents' blessing. Slowly but persistently, I was able to cajole her into a registered marriage; the social wedding could wait; it would be done only after my parents approved. And so it was that in December 1971, we signed up as husband and wife at the marriage registrar's office without anyone's knowledge. Two of my friends signed as witnesses. One of them was Altamas Kabir, who later became the Chief Justice of India.

The social marriage happened with consent from both families on the 6th of March 1973. We rented a tiny apartment near the GKW factory; we couldn't afford a better place. That year was a year of joy and despair. My father left us in September, consumed by a massive heart attack. My friend, philosopher, and guide was no more. It took me a fair while to reconcile with the reality that he was no longer among us.

But God is kind. We were gifted with a son the following year. Sitting in that damp, poorly lit apartment, our dreams soared beyond all horizons. We didn't have any savings and could just about make both ends meet with the paltry salary I earned. But as I think back, we were a happy and satisfied couple. Kamala was a source of constant courage, and she believed much more than I did that I had the ability to reach right to the top. She was my mate, my minder, my motivator, my Muse. Very often, when I would return home at the end of a tiring day's work and be required to get back to the desk at home to study accountancy, it was Kamala who kept me going with either a helping of my favourite sweets or a plate of fried prawns. I finally qualified as a cost accountant in 1974. Without Kamala, I would never have achieved what I was able to.

My jagged journeys continued, Kamala by my side. In 1977, I left GKW and joined DCM, a Delhi-based data computing firm. I had some training in computing while at GKW. Computing was a greenfield sector, new opportunities were opening up. The decision of the then industry minister, George Fernandes, to throw out the American data multinational, IBM, from India became a prod to Indian entrepreneurs to enter the field. DCM was one such firm, HCL was another. Both were competitors in an expanding business field.

Within a few months of joining DCM, I was promoted as a senior systems engineer; I had a background in Applied Physics, I took to computing like a duck to water.

Although the very mention of computers was politically unfashionable those days — they were seen as a threat to jobs — most forward-looking enterprises were quick to grasp the need to switch gears and induct the new technology. They would use the term electronic data processing instead of computers to avoid scaring or raising the hackles of workers' unions, which were very powerful in Left-ruled West Bengal at the time.

I was based out of DCM's Camac Street office. In those days, Calcutta and north Bengal were the regions I was responsible for. It was as part of one such sales foray that I first came to the offices of ABP in 1979. They were keen to acquire newly emerging work systems and initially wanted a payroll data programme written. I remember coming to the ABP offices as a DCM systems engineer and competing with a fellow engineer from HCL. We would sit side by side as we wrote our programmes, competing for the attention of the bosses at ABP. Sometimes, when I look back at the time, it seems almost surreal to me.

Anyhow, as things happened, my programme was better liked and accepted by the ABP house. But lo and behold, before I could move on to our next client in the region, I was offered a job to work with ABP. To tell the truth, I was more than a little surprised. I was not remotely a media company person. I was a trained accountant, and I was now also a computer systems engineer, but how would I fit into a media company?

But something had clicked. I was told that the "boss" — it was Arup Sarkar, or Arupbabu as I know him to this day — was very keen that I join as a senior systems analyst. I yielded, but not without negotiating my terms and negotiating them hard. I came in on what was those days considered a very good salary.

I was on my way.

A boy from a dimly-lit mofussil location in India's ill-provided northeast was on track for bigger things in the megacity called Calcutta.

2

On the Road

"Journeys, like artists, are born, and not made."

– Lawrence Durrell

I could not believe where I had landed quite suddenly. This was an entirely new space for me - a big media house, the biggest one in the region and its most prized one: *Anandabazar Patrika.* To say I was daunted would be to make an understatement. But here I was, and more awaited me as I would go along.

I couldn't even dream that day that I would be a witness to the transformation of a regional publishing house into a leading national multimedia conglomerate. Besides, I had no notion that I would play a significant role in this transformation.

Within a year of joining the ABP group, I took charge of the IT department. I was quick to understand that the key to moving ahead was modernisation. Fortunately, the top management did not require much convincing; the bosses were well in the grasp of the fast-changing media ecosystem, and they were willing to provide the required funds.

The archaic rotary printing presses were first replaced by modern offset presses. But the newsroom had to be modernised too. Journalists soon bid goodbye to typewriters and had to be trained and assisted to get used to working on keyboards attached to desktops. This may all sound simple and easily done today, but these changes were not easily achieved. What this meant was not merely a change of technology; it meant a cultural shift. And no less political - remember I am talking of the high noon of the Marxist regime in West Bengal, trade unionism was strong and often turned violent. Trade unionism was also deeply resistant to change. That was the environment in which these changes had to be managed.

I vividly remember the sense of awe and joy when the first news stories filed by our bureau in Delhi landed in Calcutta via satellite. The speed then was a mind-boggling sixty-four Kbps! Today, I grumble if the Netflix movie I want to watch gets downloaded at a speed of less than 300 Mbps.

There is another uniqueness to the ABP as a media house, which I noticed early and which I must mention: it is the culture of consciously seeking out and nurturing talent that often did not strictly have to do with the business of news-gathering. ABP prided itself as a prime pillar of culture, the arts, and literature, like a vibrant repository of the best writing talent in both Bengali and English. The ABP floors were littered with a stellar constellation of stars who were not merely the best in the field but also possessed of their peculiar eccentricities. Unforgettable characters, many of them, and I am fortunate to have shared the same workspace. The stories they were able to spot and commission, the headlines they conjured, and the displays they gave all made the *Anandabazar Patrika* and *The Telegraph*, the group's pathbreaking English daily launched in July 1982, unique market leaders.

Bijoy Chakrabarty, *Anandabazar Patrika's* news editor, was, for instance, a truly argumentative Indian. Once, I happened to inquire about his health and realised soon after that I had made a grave mistake. Because he had swung into the vortex of deep conjecture over what would happen if his health was good and what would happen were it not, how the world would be affected if he was in good health and how it would affect me if he weren't. After about ten minutes of this, I apologised to him with folded hands and took my leave.

C. P. Kuruvilla, news editor of our business daily, Business Standard, was a wizard of the newsroom. He was a chain smoker and forever wore a sly smile, disbelieving everything in the world until it passed through his lens. He loved his drink as well and would always be in high spirits past midnight. One night, he was standing stark naked in the newsroom, dictating the next day's headline.

Samaresh Bose, the legendary Bangla novelist, was the darling of ladies, and he never shied from narrating tales of his amorous escapades.

M J Akbar, firebrand editor of *The Telegraph* who later turned to politics, had his own whims and idiosyncrasies. He was once batting in a friendly office cricket match. The umpire was one of my business colleagues. Together, they had downed a bottle of vodka on the sidelines of the game. Came a time when the umpire, Akbar's drinking mate, called him out leg before. Hilarious altercations followed.

MJ refused to leave the wicket, saying, "How dare you call M J Akbar out!". The umpire, at that stage, pronounced himself king and said his ruling would hold. We had to cajole MJ into accepting the verdict.

Shakti Chattopadhyay, the legendary poet, never wrote his copy before midnight because he had to go to his favourite bar each evening. The story goes that one night, only two people were left drinking in the bar. The time, some say, was two in the morning. The other guy drinking was a double-decker bus driver. Both continued their drinking because the driver apparently assured Shakti that he would drive him home, come what may. At about three in the morning, a double-decker with two on board—the driver and Shakti—entered the narrow lane down which he lived. It was a lane that even cars of a certain size found it difficult to manoeuvre through, but the drunk driver brought a whole double-decker down. Shakti's wife was called out, and her husband duly handed over. Of course, Shakti remembered none of this.

Such were the eminences that roamed the headquarters of the venerable ABP. But they were, each of them, masters of the game, luminaries whose contribution to the publishing house and to journalism as a whole would be remembered down the generations.

* * *

Life was easy-going. The group continued to flourish. We were by far the market leaders on all counts. I found myself promoted to the post of Management Accountant, and IT reported to me. The two seemingly contrary directions my dire days of youth had pushed me in had come to coalesce. But trouble lay ahead, and in order to get to the nature of it, I must delve a little into the dominant political culture of Bengal at the time.

The Marxist-led Left Front had won a second successive term; they behaved like they were the monarchs of all they surveyed - reeking of the arrogance of power, intolerant, also feared. Our newspapers had traditionally criticised governments for their misdeeds; that's the job of a media house. We suffered for the positions we took, but we did not waver in our commitment to telling the truth. During the Emergency imposed by Indira Gandhi, two of our journalists were put behind bars.

In April 1984, the Marxist workers' union in ABP submitted a charter of demands, some of them simply absurd.

When all negotiations failed, the union, a minority group with tacit encouragement from the Left Front bosses, called a strike on April 24, 1984. Our offices and printing presses were seized. The street on which our offices stood - the famed Prafulla Sarkar Street that branches off Central Avenue - became a no-go zone for the majority of employees who wanted to work. Hooligans patrolled the road and beat up the employees who tried to approach the "sada bari", or White House, as the ABP headquarters is also known. The purpose was to create panic. This went on for fifty-one crippling days. But the strike, and its often violent nature, could not break or demoralise us.

On 14th June - it is a day I will never forget - we won a favourable court order, and employees marched to the offices under a hail of stones and brickbats. Gathered crowds cheered us on; the atmosphere was electric, and we could feel the rush of adrenaline in our bloodstreams. There was going to be no stopping us.

The police provided us with no protection, but who cared that day? The Personnel Manager was hit on the head and had to take five stitches; some others were injured in the melee, but we were riding high, like a wave. We broke open the gates, and we entered the offices; the corridors were still dark; they had become cobweb-ridden, but all of that would become the past very soon. The first decision we made upon arriving back at the workplace was that the newspapers had to come out the very next day. What followed was a tale of unbelievable camaraderie and should serve as a case study in management schools of how alignment to a common cause can create wonders. What is required is strong, lucid-headed leadership and a dedicated team that is ready to work towards a common goal.

To me, that was a historic day, a milestone in the way trade unions can be dealt with when they turn rogue and disruptive without reason.

Within hours, electricity was restored, and the presses started rolling. The newsroom was abuzz; there was excitement and activity all around. We had returned to the mother ship, and it was preparing to set sail again.

Our papers were out the next morning with the headline: "ABP employees enter their office defying armed assault." Through the traumatic period of the strike, we had been punished for what we stood for as a media group. Our delivery vans were looted daily and set on fire, and our distribution staff were beaten up. Day after day, our cameras captured the atrocities the Left-backed hooligans were wreaking on our employees. All of this and more became part of the story we told our readers. Public support grew hugely, and our circulation numbers kept rising day after day. We had to be confined to our offices for ten days because whoever tried to go out would be subjected to violence. But we put up with all of that intimidation and came out on top. The illicit persecution of the ABP house had become a national issue and condemnation of the violence against ABP employees and property rang out in Parliament.

Elections were around the corner, and the Marxists probably didn't want to get too much on the wrong side of public opinion. The way they pulled back the striking unions and unconditionally gave up demands was also demonstrative of the high prestige the ABP house is held in; you cannot mess with it beyond a point because it, too, has the force of public opinion and sympathy behind it.

* * *

I continued my climb up the ladder at work; I became second in command to Mr Ganes Nag, who headed all finance functions. He was old-school, a bit high-handed; he didn't believe in modern financial management, even things as elementary as budgetary control. What he said was the budget. After I introduced budgets as a working concept, someone asked me whether I had loosened the reins of finance and let people spend at will. Actually, what I had done was just the opposite. The then Chief Editor had lamented once that if he had to send journalists to cover a train accident in north India, he had to wait for approval from finance for the expenses. That needed to be changed; a media organisation needs to be swift on its feet because events dictate what is required to be done. Finance had not been loosened; it had been dovetailed to the requirements of our working personnel. Overnight, I became the darling of journalists.

Strike at ABP and hooliganism

Non striking employees entering ABP

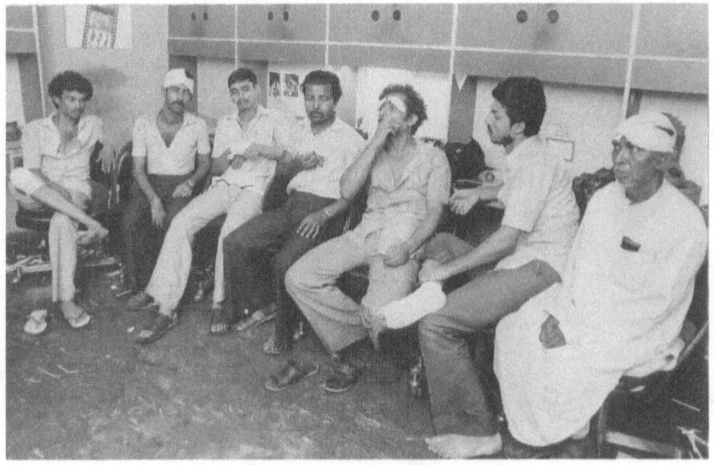

Non Striking Employees Beaten Up

ABP Employees entering the Office 14th June, 1984

ABP Van attack, 19th June, 1984

Strike at ABP and hooliganism

Strike at ABP and hooliganism

In ABP, there is a clear divide between the Church and the State, management and editorial. My effort throughout was to create a culture where one does not step onto the other, where both walk in step. Let me give you an example. In those days, the late distribution of newspapers was common and frequent. The newsroom would not finish pages early or in time, often because they were waiting to catch the news as late as possible. The press would blame the quality of newsprint for delays in printing. The advertising department would throw up its hands, saying advertisers were sending matters late, and we could not afford to lose critical revenue. We were caught in a vicious cycle of delays; every department had someone else to blame. Something had to be done.

So I broke the silo through a daily meeting -- christened 4' O clock meeting -- of all the stakeholders. The agenda was simple: to find the root cause of last night's delay and

The day violence was defeated

By M.J. Akbar

Yesterday, after a series of unusual events, the overwhelming majority of the employees of the Ananda Bazar Group of Publications managed to enter the premises which had been seized by a handful of employees backed by outsiders. This illegal closure continued for 51 days simply because the employees who wanted to work were forcibly denied entry into their office. The chief minister, Mr Jyoti Basu, himself tried his level best to find a way out of the impasse, but unfortunately his efforts to restore reason failed. Finally, the non-striking employees and the management were forced to go to the court for relief.

On Tuesday, Justice A.K. Sengupta of the Calcutta High Court ordered the administration and the police of West Bengal to remove the persons who had illegally seized the office. The police began to clear the strikers at about two in the afternoon yesterday. The employees, who had gathered to enter the office after the police had restored law and order in the area, were informed by the joint commissioner of police, Mr B.K. Basu, at 3.30 pm that they could now proceed to their office. More than 1,000 nonstriking employees, showing obvious relief, came in a procession from Waterloo Street, expecting to walk in under police protection that had become incumbent after the High Court order. Instead, they were attacked near Aliah restaurant and on Prafulla Sarkar Street itself by groups of people armed with brickbats, sodawater bottles, iron rods and lathis. Brickbats and sodawater bottles were hurled at the procession, leaving the processionists stunned and momentarily unnerved. There were injuries to 32 employees, including Mr Arun Bagchi, president of the West Bengal Union of Journalists and Mr Uma Sankar Haldar, president of the Indian Journalists' Association. Mr Parbati Mukherjee, personnel adviser to the company, who is 67 years old, received 16 stitches on his head and face in the emergency ward of the P.G. Hospital. Despite all this, the employees refused to be blackmailed by another round of violence. Showing an extraordinary—and impromptu—bravery, the employees kept moving ahead despite this hail of brickbats and sodawater bottles. In the end the overwhelming numbers of nonstrikers reached the gates and opened their office.

The striking union immediately started the canard that the office had been stormed by antisocial elements hired by the management. This falsehood was only the latest in a long line. The nonstriking employees of this company have signed a letter to the chief minister (which will be handed to him this morning) expressing their shock and anger at this accusation. They wrote and signed this letter at 7 pm to indicate that they and they alone were in the procession, and had come peacefully, without any intent of violence. In fact, in view of the order of the High Court, no one was expecting any violence. After all, the High Court had ordered the police to remove the strikers a minimum of 500 metres away from the office; so where was the question of any confrontation if the High Court order was to be fully implemented? As the employees who had come to work argued, if they had wanted to use violence why did they have to go to the High Court for an order enabling them to enter peacefully? There are more than 1,000 employees willing to take any oath anyone wants that there was no antisocial in their midst, and this propaganda is nothing but a vicious lie.

But this lie is being used to continue the physical threat to the overwhelming majority of employees who have returned to their legitimate place of work. We appeal to the government to ensure that this threat is removed and law and order is restored at once. It is a measure of our determination to continue our work, and bring out the newspapers and magazines which have been illegally shut for seven weeks, that we decided to bring out a newspaper on the very day we returned. There were enormous handicaps. The composing machines and the presses were in a state of disuse; the teleprinter lines were down. We have not been able to bring out more than a four-page edition. But we hope things will be normal tomorrow.

We hope that our readers will help us bear this attack on our right to publish by a small handful of people with ulterior motives. We have not been able to properly communicate our dilemma all this while because none of the mass-circulation newspapers of this city—*The Statesman, Amrita Bazar Patrika, Jugantar,* and *Aajkal*—have carried a single word about this unfortunate episode, not one word even mentioning that we had been arbitrarily closed down. It was an astonishing and unbelievable act of censorship. We must, however, thank those newspapers, like the *Economic Times, Sanmarg* and many other periodicals in the city and the state who reported the news. And All India Radio and Doordarshan receive our grateful thanks too for the coverage they gave.

In the end, a newspaper lives by the goodwill of its readers. Great events have taken place in our absence, and we will do our best to report and analyse them. We promise that we will not be cowed down by anyone's threats (and, of course, there are physical threats now too), and continue to work with the integrity and independence that must always exist at the heart of any newspaper. We need your support in this trying and dangerous phase of our existence.

Non-striking employees of the Ananda Bazar Group brave lathis at the crossing of Bentinck Street and Waterloo Street on Thursday

Jayewardene, PM to meet in Delhi

From Our Special Correspondent

New Delhi, June 14: The President of Sri Lanka, Mr J.R. Jayewardene, is coming here on a three-day official visit beginning June 30.

His visit, which is in response to an invitation by the Prime Minister, Mrs Indira Gandhi, will involve "an exchange of views at the highest level," according to a spokesman of the external affairs ministry here today.

The talks will focus on "traditional bilateral relations, recent developments and other matters of mutual interest."

This will be Mr Jayewardene's second meeting with Mrs Gandhi since the outbreak of ethnic violence in Sri Lanka. He was here in November during the Commonwealth Heads of Government Meeting and had detailed discussions on this issue.

The spokesman said Mr Jayewardene had agreed to visit New Delhi on his way home from London.

The Tamil issue and the mounting anti-India tirade by Sri Lankan leaders, including

Strikers pelting ABP hawkers

ANANDA BAZAR GROUP

Deadlocked

CALCUTTA, the bastion of militant trade unionism, is currently witnessing a bizarre battle between trade unions desperate to maintain their clout in the Ananda Bazar Patrika Limited, the state's largest publishing house. By last fortnight, it was evident that the battle, which was initially confined to a group of Ananda Bazar workers and the management, had become a prestige issue for the left wing trade unions and could have repercussions in industries throughout West Bengal. "The perspective of the battle has changed completely and has now become a fight for fundamental trade union rights," observed Jaygopal Roy, leader of the West Bengal Newspaper Employees Federation (WBNEF) and secretariat member of the Centre of Indian Trade Unions (CITU), the trade union wing of the CPI(M).

The change in the dimensions of the Ananda Bazar dispute began with the decision of non-striking employees and the management to assert their rights guaranteed in the Constitution and approach the courts for permission to enter their office premises. On June 12, Justice Ajit Kumar Sengupta of the Calcutta High Court ordered the state Government and the police to remove the strikers picketing the office and provide assistance to willing employees and the management to enter the office. But when journalists and other employees of Ananda Bazar marched to the office in the afternoon of June 14, the workers refused them entry and retaliated.

"The management had goondas with them and hit us first so we had to retaliate," claimed Subodh Bose, WBNEF secretary and principal correspondent in the Amrita Bazar group of publications, the main competitor of the Ananda Bazar group in the state. Whatever the reasons, the retaliation was bloody: several non-strikers had their teeth knocked out and limbs battered by lathi blows.

"But the strikers even with their lathis could not hold off the mob of employees bent upon returning to their office," said S.P. Singh, Ravivar editor. The employees successfully brought out "Extraordinary Editions" of The Telegraph and Ananda Bazar Patrika, breaking 51 days of total silence. Also, for the first time a major strike indirectly supported by the state's most powerful union had been forcibly broken by willing employees.

The implications of this for trade union leaders was obviously disturbing. "Our strike is not illegal though the management maintains otherwise. It is a protest against the management's provocative actions," explained Roy. However, what Roy did not point out was that if the Ananda Bazar management got away with what they had done, other employers could in future use loyal workers to break strikes.

The second phase of action by the strikers and their trade union supporters started almost immediately after publication was resumed. Marauding groups went about the city attacking Ananda Bazar delivery vans, assaulting hawkers going to pick up copies, tearing and burning copies snatched from hawkers and urging everybody not to buy the group's publications. Judging from the scale of operations, the attacks suggested that the strikers received help from CPI(M) and CITU cadres. While denying the intimidation, Roy claimed this was just a "working class movement and has nothing to do with the freedom of the press". The movement, it appears, justifies the beating up of non-striking employees, threatening women employees and demanding the total closure of the Ananda Bazar group of publications.

In the midst of all this, the most puzzling was the deliberate inaction of the police. Though Section 144 was imposed within 250 metres of the office the police did nothing to prevent the holding up of hawkers at the head of the road, brickbatting and squatting within the restricted area. Police officers privately admitted that they had been instructed against using tear gas or lathis to disperse demonstrators. The only job the police had been asked to do was to protect the office building, which they did. "It's not the job of the police to escort Ananda Bazar employees to their offices," said Chief Minister Jyoti Basu in defence of their inaction.

"We told the chief minister that the events in Ananda Bazar are a clear breach of law and order and it 's the responsibility of the Government to maintain law and order," said Aveek Sarkar, the managing editor of the Ananda Bazar group of publications. According to him, Jyoti Basu said he deplored the violence and gave an assurance that steps would be taken to stop it. Yet every morning hawkers are being intimidated and at times even assaulted for trying to collect the papers. "How this can go on is a mystery to me," confessed Sarkar. Subodh Bose is confident that hawkers will soon stop lifting Ananda Bazar publications.

"In this stalemate there are only two losers," remarked M.J. Akbar, editor of Sunday and The Telegraph, "the management which is losing money and the Left Front which is losing votes." The effects of this dispute, because of the involvement of all trade unions except those of the INTUC, is fast spreading to other places. All Calcutta papers suspended publication of their June 22 editions as the WBNEF called a strike in support of the Ananda Bazar cause. Employees of the Economic Times Calcutta edition were physically prevented from entering their office and one of them was also assaulted. Speaking for the trade unions, Roy declared: "We will not give up this fight and we could even resort to a state-wide strike if no solution to this impasse is found."

—INDRANIL BANERJEE

The Telegraph

CALCUTTA WEDNESDAY 20 JUNE 1984 60 PAISE

IN BRIEF

Pak denies telecast of fake film

New Delhi, June 19 (PTI): The Pakistan embassy today said there was absolutely no basis for a report of a section of the Indian Press that a fake film shown by Pakistan television had sparked off the desertion of Sikh troops in the Ganganagar area of Rajasthan.

In a news release, the embassy claimed that Pakistan had exercised utmost caution and care in reporting on the Punjab situation and refrained from telecasting any commentary as such.

"The coverage by Pakistan has been both factual and objective," it said.

The embassy said: "Pakistan television has made no film of its own on the events in the Punjab. In fact, it relayed only news clips received from the well-known international TV network, Visnews."

The Telegraph

The threats to the staff and the virtual siege of our office by antisocial elements and outsiders have made the return to normalcy even more difficult. We are not yet in a position to restore a 12-page newspaper; please accept our apologies and understand our predicament.

Ray progressing

Calcutta, June 19 (UNI): Mr Satyajit Ray, who underwent a bypass heart surgery at the Texas Heart Institute in Houston of yesterday, is progressing well, according to a report received here today.

The chief minister, Mr Jyoti Basu, now in New Delhi, asked his political secretary, Mr Ashoke Bose, to enquire about Mr Ray's condition. Accordingly, he contacted Dr K B Bakshi, who accompanied Mr Ray, and was informed that Mr Ray was progressing well.

IBRD loan for Farakka project

New Delhi, June 19 (PTI): The World Bank has extended a loan of Rs 401 crores to improve the supply of electric power in the eastern region.

According to a Bank release, the states include West Bengal, Orissa and Bihar. The loan would gain help finance the addition of 1000 MW of thermal capacity at the Farakka power plant in West Bengal at a total cost of Rs 1,100 crores.

The loan is for 20 years, including five years' grace, with a variable interest rate, currently 10.94 per cent, based on the cost of the Bank's borrowings.

Kazi joins Cong-I

Gangtok (UNI): The former chief minister of Sikkim, Kazi Lhendup Dorji's party, Sikkim United Council, has formally merged with the Congress(I).

Welcoming the merger, the state Congress(I) president said Mr Dorji's timely action would strengthen his organisation in the crucial hour. This would also help in containing regional and communal activities in the state, he said.

Iran hijackers surrender

New (AFP): Four Iranian officers who hijacked an Iranian Fokker 27 aircraft on Friday surrendered to the French police on Tuesday after authorities refused to give them political asylum.

The hijackers, along with four passengers, arrived here early on Tuesday. They hid their faces with newspapers while leaving the plane.

Waterlogging in city

By A Staff Reporter

Calcutta, June 19: A continuous downpour throughout the day today resulted in waterlogging in most parts of the city. Peak-hour traffic was stalled in central and north Calcutta while commuters returning home were greatly inconvenienced due to inadequate public transport.

Army not to withdraw fully from Golden Temple

New Delhi, June 19 (PTI): Full withdrawal of the Army from the Golden Temple complex will not be possible until all the area in the complex were fully surveyed, it was officially stated here tonight.

It was authoritatively clarified by an official spokesman that the resumption of "normal" withdrawal from the Golden Temple complex by tomorrow have been stated in the Army.

The spokesman was referring to the reported misinformation made by the Union works and housing and parliamentary affairs minister, Mr Buta Singh, that the government has decided to totally withdraw Army from the Golden Temple complex tomorrow.

The spokesman said that they had started thinning out from the Golden Temple. However, full withdrawal would not be possible until the recovery of arms from the complex, which is still going on, is complete.

There are still large quantities of explosives and arms within the temple complex, which are being recovered daily, and the resumption of normal duties at these dangerous explosives and weapons, it will not be safe to allow large number of visitors in the temple, the spokesman said.

Sikh envoy seeks asylum

Oslo, June 19 (AFP): The charge d'affaires at the Indian embassy in Oslo, Mr Maninder Singh, revealed today he had asked Norway for political asylum for himself, his wife and their three children.

At a news conference here, Mr Singh, aged 37, said he wanted to quit the Indian Foreign Service to protest against the Army action in Amritsar.

Mr Singh went to the foreign ministry this morning and asked for political asylum. The ministry told him to hand in his written statement to the police in order to keep his application for political asylum examined by the ministry of justice.

Pak sent arms to extremists

New Delhi, June 19 (PTI): Pakistan has been desperately trying to find more channels to send arms and ammunition to the Punjab extremists since March using the neighbouring flanks of Punjab, the BSF director general, Mr Birbal Nath, said here today.

A highly reliable indication of Pakistan's involvement in lending the extremists movement in Punjab was available with the BSF which, during the last four months, had detected some of their accounts and seized considerable ammunition with markings of the Pakistan ordnance factory at Wah, Mr Birbal Nath said.

Telegraph, ABP employees, vans under attack

Goons, including antisocial elements, attacking vans carrying copies of The Telegraph, Ananda Bazar Patrika and the Business Standard

Antisocials step up violence against ABP staff

By A Staff Reporter

Calcutta, June 19: Several senior employees of the Ananda Bazar group of publications were threatened and intimidated today near the office while on their way to work on a mission by a sharp rise in the number of such incidents. The early morning saw a violent attack on delivery vans and hawkers was purposes of The Telegraph and the Anandabazar Patrika.

At about 10.30 am two ladies working in the phone operating department were stopped by about 50 people near the Bengal Chemical office in Ganesh Chunder Avenue and abused and heckled. Go back today, otherwise we will make your tomorrow hell, they were told. As they were royally walking away, followed by the gang, two other employees coming by cars spotted them, took them in the taxi and drove to the Bowbazar police station, from where they came to the office with police escort.

Two other ladies working for Sunday magazine were stopped and similarly threatened in front of the GPO. They harrowly made their way into the Show Wallace office from where they rang up the ABP office. When they emerged out of the Show

On Page 5
• George Fernandes moves Press Council
• Fernandes' letter to Jyoti Basu
• Congress(I) and Congress(S) condemn attack
• Paton journalists' memo to Bhagat

Pak sent arms to extremists
...

Three marauding gangs stoning and beating passers-by during the day before launching their attacks at night.

Lanka to seek return of rebels

From Our Correspondent

Madras, June 19: One of the vital issues that the Sri Lankan President, Mr J. R. Jayewardene, and the national security minister, Mr Lalith Athulathmudali, will focus upon during their visit to New Delhi on June 19 will be the extradition of Eelam terrorists from Tamil Nadu.

Disclosing this here today, Mr S Pazaniappan, deputy Sri Lankan high commissioner, who reiterated from Colombo yesterday, the Sri Lankan government demanded the extradition of Mr Uma Maheshwaran, leader of PLOT (People's Liberation Organisation of Tamil Eelam, and Mr Padmanabha, leader of the EPRLF group, had kidnapped the Sri Lankan envoy in Jaffna.

Polls in 9 states likely next year

New Delhi, June 19 (UNI): Elections to Assemblies of at least nine states and two Union Territories will be held next year, it was learnt.

He felt that the situation would improve if the DULF leaders were to address meetings of their husbands demanding surrender and urging their clients rate to uphold it.

3 lakh hit by Assam floods

New Delhi, June 19 (UNI, PTI): The flood situation in Assam worsened today with three lakh people hit by it and several parts of northern and southern India were lashed by heavy rains, raising the water level of many rivers. Several hundred families have been rendered homeless.

Two six-year-old children were drowned in the swollen school pond of the government lower primary school in Kalamssery today.

LABOUR

Indefinite strike?

CAN any recognised union pledged to an agreement not to resort to strike on financial and economic demands before the expiry of the period stipulated in the accord, strike work and that too without notice? That is the question being asked by the management of the *Ananda Bazaar* group of publications, ever since a section of the staff went on a sudden strike on the night of April 24-25.

The events leading up to the strike began on April 24, the day of the annual general meeting of the company's employees union, which is recognised by the management. Normally, the meeting is held on the roof of the group's own Patrika House and as usual the union sought permission for the same this year too. Permission was granted with the stipulation that no outsider would be allowed. This, however, was not agreeable to the union leaders who decided to hold the meeting at a hall owned by a CPI(M)-influenced teachers' organisation in the state, about half a kilometre from Patrika House.

Posters and leaflets were distributed informing members of the new venue. The management accepted the union's decision with the proviso that while they would not stop any employee from going to the meeting, the union should ensure that normal work of the company was not affected.

But that afternoon, when the mail edition of the daily was ready for despatch, it was found that most of the drivers, loaders and peons who were needed for the despatch of the paper were not present. According to P.N. Mukherjee, personal adviser of the company, a few casual labourers were therefore engaged to do the job and the officer in charge of the motor vehicles department himself drove a van to the railway station.

In the meantime, a few drivers and peons rushed back to the office and on seeing the group of casual workers doing the job they were meant to do, raised serious objections. Pandemonium soon broke out and the officer in charge of the motor vehicles department, who had just returned from the station, was beaten up. And a brawl ensued.

Attempts were made to settle the issue amicably but the union leaders then intervened and demanded suspension of the department in-charge. The management refused and offered to negotiate the next day, but the union stuck to its guns. And at midnight, while the offset plates were being taken for printing, irate union members destroyed the plates. Journalists and non-journalists were told to leave the building. The strike had begun.

Not a single publication of the group hit the stands the next day. And employees who turned up for work were forcibly not allowed to report for duty. Later, five journalists and 47 non-journalist employees of the company lodged complaints with the local police against union members accusing them of assault and physical humiliation.

By the afternoon of April 25, Prafulla Sarkar Street where the publishing house has its headquarters had the look of a fort under siege. Except for those supporting the strike, no one was even allowed to enter the street. Posters soon came up saying that the union had been forced to resort to an indefinite strike due to the intransigent attitude of the management to their 16-point demand including that of grant of pension.

The management took the stand that

the existing agreement, due to expire in early 1985, specifically forbids a strike in support of economic demands. The union meanwhile distributed pamphlets highlighting the demand for pension. The original demand of suspension of the department in-charge was forgotten.

Aveek Sarkar, editor of the *Ananda Bazaar Patrika*, the leading Bengali daily, told THE WEEK " We cannot honour an illegal strike and sit with the union for negotiation". On the other hand, Sushil Nath Kar, joint secretary of the employees union said "the day the company would agree just to discuss the pension issue, the strike would be lifted. We don't want any prior commitment on this count. We want only that the Sarkars would agree to sit with us".

In that case, what about the other demands? "Those are all secondary to the issue of pension", replied Kar. Kar had no satisfactory reply when asked why, in that case, those other demands had been raised at all and about the existing agreement.

Sarkar and M.J. Akbar, editor of *The Telegraph* and *Sunday*, met Chief Minister Jyoti Basu prior to his visit to China seeking his help in ending the strike. Nothing concrete was accomplished. Also, several round of meetings have taken place between the Labour Minister K.P. Ghosh and representatives of the management and union. But all in vain.

Meanwhile, a large majority of the non-journalist employees and all the journalists working for the group have formed a joint action committee to try and resolve the strike. The committee has been organising processions and street corner meetings throughout the city appealing to the state government to end the strike. Almost all the big names of the group, editors Santosh Kumar Ghosh and Nirendra Nath Chakravarty, and well-known writers like Barun Sengupta, Arun Bagchi, Sunil Gangopadhyay and Sirshendu Mukherji addressed public meetings, narrating how the publications of the group came to a halt.

In their meetings, *Ananda Bazaar* employees have highlighted the fact that none of the other publications in the state have written anything about the strike. "Today or tomorrow *Ananda Bazaar* is bound to reopen. And if by any chance misfortune ever stalks those houses, we must show them that we are not so ungracious as they are now to us", M.J. Akbar told his audience.

Stating their case. M.J. Akbar addressing a street-corner meeting

—TAPASH GANGULY

to make sure responsibility was fixed and the mistake never repeated. The news editor was made the Chair of these meetings. I would intervene anytime this group needed my help. Believe me, it worked wonders, and the newspapers stopped being late. What was required was an understanding between department heads of each other's problems and a collective will to sort them out. What was required was a sense that everybody was playing on the same team, not competing against each other. I believe that most problems faced in the corporate world can be solved by understanding, empathy and the willingness to listen.

* * *

I was a high performer, and no question could be raised about my performance. I say this not as a brag but as a matter of pride. One should be able to take pride in one's work; that is one of the things that keeps you motivated and focused on performing even better.

One day, I was asked by the management whether I was confident enough to take full charge of finance. I wasn't about to say no. I was promoted overnight to Head of Finance and IT. Mr. Ganes Nag, my martinet boss, went on a couple of years' leave until he retired. He was a chain smoker. He was suffering from pneumonia. Last year, as I was sitting by his bedside at the hospital, he held my hands and promised he would never smoke after his return home. He never returned. It was a poignant parting. I still hold a lot of respect for this tragic hero of mine from whom I learned a lot.

As Head of Finance, I joined the Top Management Committee (TMC). It consisted of the Strategic Business Unit (SBU) and function heads and was headed by the Managing Director. The TMC would meet once a month. Members of the TMC were allowed to travel Business Class. The fare was high, almost two times the price of an Economy Class ticket. I didn't believe that was value for money; I continued travelling Economy even when some of my other TMC colleagues would be flying Business Class. I preferred keeping a low profile. Much later, when I took over as Managing Director and CEO, my boss persuaded me to travel Business Class as I was by then also the face of ABP to the outside world.

A new chapter dawned on my life. My interactions with banks and financial institutions increased substantially. Modernisation was my goal, and funds were required to pour in through a variety of instruments. Our new printing establishment was set up ten kilometres away from our office with a pre-owned press imported from Taiwan. It was of the same brand and model as our existing presses. But it was almost unused. This decision was one of the most prudent ones. This was the press that churned out its first copy when fire engulfed our building and destroyed almost everything. I shall narrate that story to you later.

We were soon printing our newspapers in colour, and the numbers had to be upscaled without any compromise on quality. We were acquiring the best of the best from the world; we were able to get better and bigger all the time.

The company's financials also improved substantially. Unlike in the past, we have become more bottom-line-oriented. Underperformance was challenged, and we weeded out a substantial number of underperformers under a voluntary separation programme. We retained McKinsey to develop new strategies for cost reduction by removing non-value-adding activities. An easy-going organisation was transforming into a goal-oriented modern corporation.

In 1991, Narasimha Rao took over as the Prime Minister. Manmohan Singh, the renowned economist and former Governor of the RBI, joined the cabinet as the Finance Minister. The duo opened the doors of the Indian economy through a slew of radical decisions to liberalise. Those decisions would have a cascading impact across the board, including on the media industry, but that is an entirely different story. We, as a media organisation, were smart enough to recognise the new opportunities that were coming our way. Our all-round growth continued.

* * *

Disaster struck in the wee hours of September 4, 1999, when a massive fire gutted our offices, our beloved "sada bari". The fourth floor collapsed into the third. Two of our employees died. The inferno raged for two days; the flames licked away everything, and what they spared was washed away by fire brigade water cannons. Some of us just couldn't stand and watch the devastation. I realised that our computer servers and many desktops were housed on the second floor. I knew that if we lost the server room, we would have nothing to fall back on. I led a small IT team into the building to recover the servers and desktops. We were in a dire emergency; desperate measures were required. We had to respond, and the first step required was to relocate the servers and a handful of desktops to set up a network in our classified advertisement offices just across the road. The fire services personnel did not want us to take the risk; they feared the third floor would collapse, too, and we would get trapped. But we had no option. We were obstinate. We had to take the risk and set up a temporary network with what we could rescue from the wreckage of the second floor.

It took us the better part of the day, but we were able to set up a temporary office and functioning newsroom by the evening. Our newspapers came out, as usual, the next morning: "ABP rises like a Phoenix from the ashes" ran the headline. We proceeded this way from our temporary workstations for two weeks until we rented two floors of a nearby building and resumed a relatively more normal and elaborate operation.

It took us a whole year to rebuild and restore our headquarters. My boss at the time, Shobha Subrahmanyan, was an iron lady. She would never compromise on quality. She was meticulous in her work. She would delve deep into any problem and was never satisfied until she had worked everything out. She was a hard taskmaster; office folks treated her with a sense of awe and respect.

I had a central role to play in the physical and psychological rebuilding of the organisation after the devastating fire, and I have a sense that what I did during and after the fire was not only noted but also deeply appreciated. In 2001,

The gutted third floor of ABP Pvt. Ltd.
Dated: 5th September, 1999

The gutted third floor of ABP Pvt. Ltd.
Dated: 5th September, 1999

The gutted third floor of ABP Pvt. Ltd.
Dated: 5th September, 1999

Fire rages in the office of ABP Pvt. Ltd.
Dated: 4th September, 1999

Rs 1.50 · CALCUTTA SATURDAY 4 SEPTEMBER 1999 · INTERNET EDITION: http://www.telegraphindia.com

Fire engulfs our home

ABP employee dies in 10-hr blaze

WE SHALL OVERCOME

A crisis or a disaster is always disheartening. But it is also a challenge. A challenge before the institution facing the crisis and before the human beings who work in that institution. The ABP group faced such a crisis early on Friday morning when a fire devastated the entire third floor of its premises. But the fact that readers this morning are able to read the **Anandabazar Patrika** and **The Telegraph** is the best evidence that the crisis has been met and the challenge successfully overcome. It is a matter of pride and a sign of the commitment of the ABP group to its wide and loyal readership that the two dailies are available in the market this morning.

There is sorrow and gloom at the pieces of history and hard work which have been destroyed by the fire but the prevailing mood is not informed by pessimism but by a determination to work against the odds and to honour the commitment to readers to be the first and best with news and views. In the literal sense, this has been the ABP group's trial by fire; the mood is of rising from the ashes.

> Stepping over the trail of destruction and shock that the fire left in its wake required an act of will. Today's edition epitomises that act of will ... This consciousness is the driving force which is in your hands this morning.

The determination and the optimism are rooted firmly in history. This is not the first crisis that the ABP group has faced in its long and distinguished career. Sarojini Naidu was present at the birth of the group and the latter always felt in those heady days the wrath of the British government. If that threat was overcome by the spirit of nationalism, it was courage that enabled the group to stand above the oppression and the pettiness of the Emergency. Political combativeness and discrimination are things that the ABP group has learnt to live with and even, perhaps, to enjoy. But a fire is a danger of a different kind. It is not within the realms of the expected. It strikes without any warning. This is where Friday's menace was radically different from the previous threats that have hovered over the ABP house. Stepping over the trail of destruction and shock that the fire left in its wake required an act of will. Today's edition epitomises that act of will.

An act of will, according to most philosophers, is a reflection of a consciousness. For The Telegraph, what is that consciousness? It is the commitment to meet the expectations of readers and well-wishers. It is the commitment to stand above calamity and sorrow, even one's own, and to remain true to one's calling. It was this consciousness that was writ large over the faces of all who work in The Telegraph as they stood transfixed by the horror of the inferno that engulfed the top half of the building in which they work. This consciousness is the driving force which is in your hands this morning.

The Telegraph has promises to keep, pledges to honour. Working against odds and with limited resources, were constraints that the fire imposed. The drive to overcome the consequences of the fire originated from the desire to keep the promises and the pledges. The fire destroyed part of the building but it has served to rejuvenate in The Telegraph the determination to do better, to overcome challenges. Grim with **The Telegraph**, the best is yet to be.

BY A STAFF REPORTER

Calcutta, Sept. 3: A massive blaze ravaged the top floor of ABP Limited's four-storeyed building in central Calcutta early this morning. One employee died of suffocation.

Another employee was mopping till late this evening. The fire brigade said it is too early to ascertain the cause of the fire or the extent of damage. Thirty-six fire tenders fought the blaze for nearly 10 hours and brought it under control at 3 pm.

The third floor houses the editorial office of the 77-year-old **Anandabazar Patrika** and the circulation, advertisement and accounts departments of the company. Scores of journals and historical documents in the second floor library have been damaged.

All the departments housed on the third floor have been reduced to ashes, including computers and other equipment. Only last year the editorial office of **Anandabazar Patrika** was completely renovated and computerised. The building was constructed in the early 30s.

The forensic department will investigate the fire.

Employees first noticed smoke emanating from the lift around 1.30 am. Ashish Majumdar, a photographer with **Anandabazar Patrika**, recounted the incident. "I was on the second floor when I saw the lift covered by a coil of smoke. I opened the lift-gate and thick smoke came rushed in."

He rushed down the stairs to the ground floor and alerted guards. "I then went to the reception. I thought that all the telephone lines would be down. Luckily, the phones were still working and I informed the fire brigade and Lalbazar," he said.

Thick curls of smoke billowed from the building when the fire brigade arrived around half-an-hour later. In minutes, orange-yellow flames were leaping out of the north-western side of the third floor. They flickered and danced from one window to another as fire personnel set up their gear.

The blaze spread quickly and the flames licked the building, which was now enveloped by thick, black smoke. Firemen, some wearing masks, entered the building while a turn-table ladder spread water on the inferno.

The heat was intense and the smoke was choking us. We found it extremely difficult to fight the fire," said a fire brigade personnel. A stench-burning smell wafted across as employees, who had arrived from all corners of the city on hearing the news, watched in disbelief.

Driven by a gentle breeze, the flames raced through the third floor, gutting the offices. Just as the fire brigade thought it had the blaze under control, black smoke would emerge from a corner. "The flames seem to be playing hide and seek. We douse one side and minutes later, there's smoke on another side," said a fire fighter.

Calcutta Municipal Corporation officers joined in the operation. Armed with large hammers, they went to the third floor and smashed windows to let the noxious fumes out. White smoke gushed out of the smashed windows and fire personnel reached deep into the third floor, spraying water.

The ominous sign of black smoke appeared on the terrace and the flames wreaked further havoc as the third floor roof cracked and caved in. Columns of black smoke curling out of the building could be seen as far as from Howrah bridge. The intense heat cracked windows, which were reduced to shards by little explosions.

Around 12.30 pm, fire brigade personnel carried out Kinkar Kumar Jana, a peon who had voluntarily stayed back on the third floor reportedly to attend to phone calls. He was rushed to Calcutta Medical College and Hospital where he was declared brought dead.

Kamal Kumar Samanta had a close shave. "I woke up when I thought I was choking. I was in the north-western side of the building. I saw the fire rush towards me and panicked because all routes were blocked.

"I knew that I had to get out. I also realised that no one would come to my rescue amidst the shouts for help around me. The next second I remembered that there used to be a rope in the room. I would have to take my chances. So I secured the rope firmly and then looked below. With a silent prayer on my lips, I caught the rope tightly and then slid down," he said.

Even as he recounted his miraculous escape, firemen continued to battle. The fire engines emptied their water tanks, drove to the ABP fire point to refill and returned. Fire personnel relentlessly continued to douse the stubborn blaze.

■ Another report on Page 6

Fire rages in the office of ABP Ltd on Friday morning. *Picture by Amit Datta*

Loyal till the last

BY A STAFF REPORTER

Kinkar Kumar Jana, a peon on duty on the third floor, is the only person to have died in the blaze at the offices of ABP Ltd that broke out early Friday morning. Five persons, including two firemen, were injured.

Aged 50, Kinkar hailed from Baikthai Narendra village near Digha in Midnapore. He was associated with the company for almost 20 years having started his work at the "Town" section of the circulation department. He was assigned to the third floor some months ago.

According to reports, Kinkar, who was one of the peons responsible for the safe custody of the chief editor's room, was sleeping when the fire started at around 2 am.

He was woken up by the commotion down the corridor on the western side of the building. He was in a room next to the chief editor's office on the eastern side. Seeing that the blaze was at a distance, he reportedly stayed back in the room to answer phone calls.

But the blaze and the smoke spread rapidly and he apparently became unconscious because of the suffocating smoke.

He was brought out from the building in this state by firemen and rushed to the hospital, where he was pronounced dead.

Kinkar is survived by his wife and two children. He was known to be a conscientious and loyal worker — the fact that he did not leave the office when he could have indicates this.

Kinkar, whose left hand was affected by polio in childhood, was brought in the ABP fold when he was 17 years old.

> **The Telegraph** today is a truncated 12-page edition because of the fire in our office. We hope our readers will bear with us.
>
> We have shifted our operations to 14 Madan Street. Our new numbers are: The Telegraph-2216604, 2216605, Anandabazar Patrika-2376000, 2216600, Advt-2376768, 2307588, Fax-2300160

It will take more than a fire to stop ABP from functioning

Smells like team spirit

VIR SANGHVI

On a Sunday, two days after our office building has been devastated by perhaps the worst fire that Calcutta has seen for many years, you will forgive me if I indulge in a little nostalgia, a little sentiment and — inevitably — a little trumpet-blowing.

The trumpet-blowing, first. As you probably know, having read the newspapers and watched television, the fire was so severe that two floors of the building were gutted and our office is still uninhabited, largely because we are waiting to make sure that no part of the roof is going to collapse or that there is no serious structural damage. Despite that, you are holding a copy of *The Telegraph*. More to the point the paper came out yesterday because the editorial team worked all night from a small alternative location to ensure that readers got their morning dose of *The Telegraph*. Even more impressive, *Anandabazar Patrika*, whose offices are located on a floor that was devastated, produced an edition yesterday.

I can say all this without embarrassment because I can claim no credit for any role in this enterprise. I was in Mumbai when the fire broke out and the nearest I got to the smoke was while watching Star News. Besides, it wasn't just the journalists who contributed to this astonishing achievement. It was the whole organization. Special mention must be made of the computer boffins who managed to put together an alternative network in a remarkably short time so that the papers could be produced.

Anybody who works for ABP will concede not everything is perfect in the organization. But of two things there can be no doubt. One: it is one of the few outfits in Calcutta that has a product that is world class.

And two: despite the fancy innovations, the identity cards that open the doors, the state of the art computer system and whatever, the real strength of ABP is the people. The only reason the papers came out on Saturday despite the devastation is that the people in this organization worked as a team.

That is why people like me always say that once you work for ABP, it becomes almost impossible to work for anybody else.

It is hard to be sentimental about a squat, ugly building where the majority of us have no alternative but to work in windowless rooms. But strangely, when I saw black smoke emanating from the roof, I put off the television, unable to watch any longer. My god, I thought to myself, I must be getting old if the sight of that building brings tears to my eyes.

I remember the building well. I first saw it in 1986 when I came to Calcutta to negotiate with Aveek Sarkar for a job as editor of *Sunday*. On the phone, Aveek was delightfully vague about all the details. What time did he expect to see me? What was the address? And so on.

"Don't worry," he said dismissively, "just tell the driver you want to go to ABP and he'll bring you here."

The taxi driver I hired at the Grand did not know what ABP stood for. Ananda Bazar Patrika, I said helpfully.

"*Amrita Bazar*"? He asked.

That couldn't be right. I consulted the letterhead on the note Aveek had written me "Prafulla Sarkar Street," I said.

"Sarkar?" He was completely befuddled.

Help was at hand in the shape of Aruna Paul, an old friend, who I saw emerging from the Grand. "Tell me where Aveek's office is," I implored. Paul went into a hasty consultation with the two ladies who accompanied her. Finally, they explained the way to the driver. Though I spoke no Bengali, I could tell that they were directing him to a newspaper office. I caught the words "central avenue".

My driver was charged with a new motivation. Darting in and out of the Chowringhee traffic, he rushed past Metro and broke a red light before turning right to deposit me at an old and impressive building.

Silly man, I thought, how could he have not known where this was? I paid him and entered the building. Where, I asked the watchman, did Aveek Sarkar sit? He looked at me as though I was mad. Other people came to stare at me. There were whispered conversations. Finally, they broke the bad news to me.

The driver had dropped me at Statesman House.

I walked the rest of the way thinking to myself that when Aveek Sarkar declared that Ananda Bazar was one of the five great media institutions of the world, he may have been exaggerating slightly.

In those days, the ABP office looked much as it does now — or at least as it did before the fire. Only, it was less hi-tech and — how does one put this delicately? — less *upmarket*. There were no computers and Aveek operated not from the plush suite he has now, complete with Chesterfield sofas and Rosenthal crockery (miraculously, even though the rest of the third floor burnt down, Aveek's office was untouched — obviously, the fire god recognizes a Chesterfield when he sees one) but from an unattractive little room where you couldn't see the furniture because the entire space was covered with important papers that he had neglected to sign for several years. (He still doesn't sign them but they are now stored in somebody else's room.)

What gave it a special character, however, were the bearers. I had come from Mumbai (then Bombay) where peons wore sparkling uniforms and saluted smartly. What a change therefore to find bearers who wore long shirts and *dhotis*, acknowledged you with a cursory shake of the head and looked, for all the world, like down at heel poets who hoped to get Ananda Publishers to give them a break!

Over the years, however, I learnt to respect the bearers. They may not have conformed to multinational standards, but they were as integral a part of the organization as the editors (actually, considering the editors were people like myself, they were probably more integral to the organization). They knew their jobs — some like Shivu, my bearer could probably have done my job — and they demonstrated the kind of loyalty that keeps ABP going.

It was tragic but not entirely surprising that the one person who died in the fire was one of Aveek's bearers. Though the truth is difficult to establish, some accounts have it that he refused to leave the third floor till it was too late, because he felt that it was his job to try and help.

What else do I remember about the building? I remember the canteen which managed the difficult feat of sprinkling sugar on the omelette sandwiches. (After two such sandwiches, I started sending Shivu to Amber to get my lunch) I remember the buzz that used to go down the corridors when Aparna Sen or Tiger Pataudi — both ABP editors — would walk to their offices. I remember the near riot that occurred in 1990 when Aveek invited Amitabh Bachchan to take tea with ABP's editors. The riot came as a shock to both men. Aveek refused to accept that his employees would not meekly disperse once he told them to. And Amit, who was going through one of his cyclical bad phases, was thrilled to find that he could still generate this kind of hysteria.

I remember the old motor vehicles department (now replaced by a new motor vehicles department across the street), run by a dodgy old codger whose manner suggested that each time he sanctioned a car, his heart missed a beat. I remember my office which became something of a tourist attraction in the building because nobody could understand why I had done it up entirely in black and white.

But enough sentiment. By Monday or Tuesday, the windowless rooms at 6 Prafulla Sarkar Street will probably be occupied again. The whirr of computers, the jangle of telephone rings, the beeps of the fax machines and the tantrums of temperamental writers will once again fill the walls of the building. And yes, we'll be back to complaining about the canteen, bitching about motor vehicles and hassling the artroom to finish our pages.

When you work for ABP you realize that it takes more than a fire to stop this organization from functioning.

Suspended animation

I was promoted to Chief Operating Officer, which meant I now headed all operations except HR, Sales, and marketing. I was allotted a nice corner room in the new office. My workload increased manifold. I spent many sleepless nights in the printing rooms trying to understand how these huge presses churn out newspapers at the blinding speed of 45,000 copies an hour. My interactions with the company's blue-collar workers increased. The idea was two-fold: to gain the trust of the workforce and to learn the technology of printing from the ground level.

I arrived at the presses as a novice, but with the help of press workers, I began to understand the science and art of printing. In 2002, we imported a state-of-the-art printing press capable of churning out 70,000 newspaper copies per hour. We installed it at our Salt Lake facility in the suburbs. That is when we shut down printing operations at our Prafulla Sarkar Street headquarters. We then started setting up multiple printing facilities in order to reach readers in far corners each morning. Technology helped. We were now able to design and lay out our newspapers in Calcutta and transmit them electronically over high-speed lines for remote printing. This also meant that editorially, our newspapers did not need to be Calcutta-centric anymore; a lot of micro-level news began to be covered, and our readers loved that. We realised that this was the way to go.

There was no dearth of information; the issue was how soon we could process it and put it out to our readers. At that time, any information needed was churned out by the central IT department, and often, the process impeded swift decision-making. I felt the dire need to plan our resources anew. I decided to implement SAP, a super-speed software application, across the organisation. We chose the German multinational Siemens as our implementation partner and implemented SAP in February 2002. SAP had just announced a product dedicated to media requirements called IS-MAM. We were the first media house in Asia to import and implement it. Even today, the backbone of our information network is SAP. Overnight, we decentralised the IT department, and information was at the fingertips of the employees. Decision-making became fast and easy. That was a landmark for ABP. We recruited high-quality IT personnel. A new information era had been inaugurated.

In 2002, twenty-five years of Marxist rule in Bengal were celebrated with great fanfare. Due to their radical and violent trade unionism, most industries had left Bengal for better pastures. Once highly industrialised, Bengal had turned barren. The jute mills that lined the banks of the river Hooghly were all closed as the state lost its most profitable cash crop. Bengal was the centre of India's automobile and engineering industries. They, too, shut shop because of the hostile political atmosphere and moved to other states. By 2002, we could barely name a couple of industries. Real estate developers acquired huge factory floors for a song; a large number of multi-storied housing projects for low and middle-income families got underway. But none of this was going to create wealth. This was also the time that the exodus of young talent from Bengal began, especially in the IT sector. Young people began to drift in droves to Bangalore and Hyderabad, the new and vibrant IT hubs.

As the millennium drew to a close, another troubling prospect loomed — mankind needed to rewrite billions and billions of computer codes which didn't recognise any year beyond 1999. The problem was christened Y2K.

There was a worldwide dearth of qualified IT personnel to handle such a massive undertaking. Rumour-mongering turned into apprehensions over the collapse of a world completely dependent on computer technology, even worse. People started believing that at the stroke of midnight, the world would come to a standstill. Nothing would work, and a disaster of unforeseen proportions would be triggered. The fear of Y2K was such that most believed we were heading for a catastrophe on New Year's Day. I recall I was on a flight to Calcutta from Singapore on the night of December 31, 1999. Some of my friends and well-wishers were apprehensive about me and asked me not to take the risk of flying that night — come the turn of the millennium and the computer systems would all collapse, there's danger, they warned. But all of that was illogical; I never paid any attention to any of it. We landed safely in Calcutta a little past midnight; I did hear a few murmurs of relief in the aircraft cabin as we came to a halt.

* * *

One of the turnaround moments of the Indian IT industry was waking up from slumber and taking the lead in sorting issues arising from the complex Y2K problem.

This became a unique example of transformation and growth by grabbing the right opportunity at the right time. It would remain a lesson to every corporate. Indian IT personnel worked all over the world and by the turn of the millennium, almost all the critical 20th-century programmes were made 21st-century compatible. The task was huge with billions of lines of code to be rewritten.

But the good part of it was that the Indian IT industry got a shot in the arm and transformed itself almost overnight into a global leader. Many Indian IT companies flourished — Infosys, TCS, WIPRO, and Cognizant became household names.

Bengalis were known for their intellect and preference for white-collar jobs. Here was a situation tailor-made for them, a perfect match. Hundreds, then thousands, of young and talented Bengalis joined large and not-so-large IT companies, which were mostly based in the South. The exodus continues to this day, so much so that Bengal often resembles a home for the elderly. The young generation has either migrated abroad, mostly to the USA, or they are working in the humming IT hubs of Gurgaon, Pune, Hyderabad, and Bangalore.

Looking at the general drift of things in Bengal, particularly from the business and corporate point of view, I decided to do a SWOT analysis of our state:

Strengths:

- English-educated high-intellect youth
- Lower salary compared to other Metros

- Lower Cost of living
- People turnover one of the lowest in the country
- The wish of the workforce to come home and stay with ageing parents
- A reformed Marxist government ready to embrace change

Weaknesses:

- The negative perception among industrialists
- Delay in decision-making by Bengal bureaucracy
- Doubts about the good intentions of the government
- Radical trade unionism

Opportunities:

- More profitable business due to low salary cost.
- Better business opportunities due to closeness to China and the Far East.
- Cheaper land compared to any other big city.
- Recruitment opportunities of the best candidates from the famous institutes like IIT Kharagpur, ISI Kolkata, IIM Kolkata, and XLRI Jamshedpur.

Threats:

- Frequent Strikes and Bandhs by the trade unions.
- The cost of withdrawal and relocation of business.
- Unwillingness of Senior people moving to Calcutta, believing it to be a retrograde step in their career.

After this exercise was done, I began to plan an Annual IT Exhibition and Conference in Calcutta, which I named INFOCOM. I went around the country to sound out some of my old friends in the IT sector who were now CEOs or Presidents of large IT companies. Everyone discouraged me. Some called it utopian. An IT conference in Calcutta? It would be a complete flop.

Failure, or the intimidation of it, always made me more adamant and determined; this was true of me since I was a schoolboy, and we shall presently come to a childhood episode that would illustrate it.

As I flew back to Calcutta, I had made my decision. INFOCOM would happen at any cost. I decided that the event would be organised by drawing on our own resources. The following week, I flew to Delhi and convinced Kiran Karnik, the then-President of NASSCOM, to partner with us. NASSCOM was the apex IT industry association. They, too, organised a number of IT conferences. But they had no footprint in the East. I explained my SWOT analysis of Bengal to him and convinced him about how NASSCOM stood to gain from the partnership. After a long discussion, he agreed.

My next task was to convince the IT minister of Bengal. Mr. Manab Mukherjee was a very open-minded person. He agreed almost immediately and sanctioned the government-owned Netaji Indoor Stadium as the venue for INFOCOM. I have yet to meet such a minister — so hands-on, dynamic, a man who believed in leading from the front.

I painted a picture of a dream Bengal abuzz with IT industries and made him believe that INFOCOM would play a lead role in the state's transformation. I was successful because of my conviction. Five years later, ABP was recognised by the government of West Bengal for its outstanding contribution to Bengal's IT industry.

But let me first narrate the spectacular journey of INFOCOM. The event would turn twenty this year. After I had done the SWOT exercise, I started visiting Bangalore every fortnight to market and sell INFOCOM. Many a time, Manab Mukherjee accompanied me. During our meetings with the CEOs of large IT companies, he expressed his government's sincere desire to bring in IT investments into Bengal and that he would remove any hurdles that might come in the way. He highlighted the strengths and opportunities of investing in Bengal. His sincerity impressed them. Once, during my meeting at a large IT company in Bangalore, the CEO complained that the government had promised land in Calcutta for their new office, but that had not come about. Such was my rapport with the minister that I called his office and reported the matter. The promised land was sanctioned then and there. These incidents built confidence among the IT companies that Calcutta could be a good destination for investment.

The first INFOCOM was a runaway success. Around 20 IT companies sponsored the event. Speakers came from all over India and abroad. It was inaugurated by Mr Pramod Mahajan, the then Union IT Minister. The exhibition stalls had huge footfalls, and the sponsors were happy with the response. Calcutta had never experienced an event so elaborately and meticulously planned and staged. I was certain that this event would go a long way.

The venues became bigger every passing year, and sponsors almost touched the hundred mark. Not a single large or medium IT company was absent at INFOCOM. Revenues doubled every year. Around 1000 delegates and more than 100 speakers from India and all over the world participate every year at INFOCOM. It has become a familiar and well-known brand in India.

The state government allotted IT enterprises a special zone called Sector V in the suburb of Salt Lake, close to the airport. Most of the large IT companies started operating from there. Today, more than two hundred thousand IT professionals work in Calcutta alone. This number would be much higher if we take into account all of Bengal. I could not believe that one event could catalyse such a massive movement. If I were to analyse today what made this happen, I would say our sky-high aspirations, conviction, determination, and uncompromising quality were the reasons.

But, as with most initiatives, some pitfalls lay ahead. NASSCOM decided to close the partnership as they were not getting the desired value out of it. That day, I determined that we needed to partner with the largest event company in the world. The name was undoubtedly CeBIT of Hanover in Germany. I made an appointment with the CEO of CeBIT and flew to Germany. It didn't take long to convince Ernst Rowe, the CEO, to partner with us. That year, INFOCOM happened in Hyderabad in partnership with CeBIT. This taught me that any target, however difficult it may seem, is achievable. I carried this belief throughout my life, and every time, it rewarded me.

* * *

In 2000, I was sent by the company for a Leadership Development Programme organised by the London Business School. The programme was based on 360-degree feedback. This programme was to trigger deep introspection in me about bringing about some radical behavioural changes. The broad sum of the feedback I received in the programme was that I was a high performer and a taskmaster but almost a cut-and-dried robot. I was an introverted backroom boy, and my people skills needed significant improvement. People were scared of me. I wouldn't say it was a shocker to me. But the intensity with which the feedback hit me left me startled. I decided to consciously change myself on my return.

I started meeting my peers, very often without any fixed agenda. I had to be smart and dexterous about this, lest someone smelt a rat.

I started opening up to their ideas. I realised that many of them were good ideas. For instance, I couldn't find any financial justification to launch multiple remote editions. I realised that it had far deeper ramifications. The readers should be at the centre of our canvas. Readers wanted the stories from their backyard, not the ones that are happening in the city of Calcutta.

I yielded and sanctioned funds. Today, one of the prime reasons why the Indian newspaper industry is still thriving is because we are so hyper-local. Google has not yet found a weapon to fight this. I am sure they will someday.

I also tried to go the extra distance to familiarise myself with the lives of my colleagues outside the workspace—their families, their hobbies and interests, their joys and despairs. I was trying to transform myself. Today, I can boast that I am loved by one and all at ABP because I never failed their trust. There have been disagreements, but once a decision had been made, I took it to the very end. I was overwhelmed by the emotions of my colleagues, some of whom I had rarely ever met, on the day of my farewell.

As I moved on in my career, most of my peers began to report to me. Some were even my seniors. Believe me, I never faced any problem in leading them and getting the best performance out of them. This is a difficult problem for many. But I succeeded because I was fair. I cannot recall a single incident when I was unfair to someone. Sometimes, they were angry with me, but I stuck to my principles, and someday, in the future, they will confide that I made the right decision. A true leader must be fair and trustworthy. In many instances, I was ruthless because I had to be because there was no better way out. I hated mediocrity and always pursued excellence. I reminded my team that only three things matter. Setting seemingly unbelievable targets, having conviction in them and leaving no stone unturned to achieve them. I have seen this happen in my life umpteen times. That doesn't mean I never failed. I probably failed more than I succeeded. But failure made me more adamant. I come now to the promised example from my schoolboy days.

I was an easy-going student. We lived, as I have told you, in a remote and mofussil town called Hailakandi in Assam. Often, I would take my eyes off my studies. I failed in Mathematics in my eighth standard finals. I was so afraid of my parents that I hid the answer paper in a pigeonhole in the house adjacent to ours. My mother was by then the Assistant Headmistress of the local girls' school. One of her colleagues informed her that our results had been published. She came home and asked for my answer paper. I remember the beating I got from my father that day—for failing the Mathematics exam as well as for not telling the truth. I was only 11 years old. But that day was a lesson I have never forgotten.

I got engrossed in studies in my six-by-six room for prolonged hours. I stood second in class in the standard nine exams. In standard 10, I selected, as a challenge, Mathematics as my second elective subject. My board exam was due in the summer of 1961. I remained cloistered in my little study till late every night. I remember it was the centenary year of Rabindranath Tagore's birth. The whole town was out attending cultural programmes. My parents requested a respite for a day. But I didn't agree. In the board exam, I stood first in the school, got around 90% marks in both Mathematics papers and received a gold medal for scoring the highest marks in Sanskrit from the district. I carried this perseverance until the final day of my executive life. I preached to my team that they should never be afraid of failure and keep on innovating.

* * *

Shobha resigned in 2000 to look after her ailing parents in Bangalore. For some time, she worked from both cities, but that didn't work out.

ABP always believed in good governance. Our board was anyone's envy. It was chaired by Dr. Ashok Ganguly, the retired Unilever India Chairman. The Audit Committee was chaired by R. Gopalakrishnan, a board member of Tata Sons, the controlling company of the Tata Empire. Other members were Dr Bimal Jalan, the retired Governor of the Reserve Bank of India, Ranjit Pandit, Country head of McKinsey, Shobha Subrahmanyan and the two promoter brothers Aveek Sarkar and Arup Sarkar.

After Shobha's early retirement, the board appointed Mr. Aniruddha Lahiri, another Unilever veteran, to take over the reins of the company as the Managing Director. I called him Ani, and he called me Purki. He joined in 2001 and served for five years. He depended on me a lot. He brought in a culture of accountability. The performance management system he implemented was excellent and very similar to the one being followed by Unilever. The corridors of ABP became witness, for the first time, to a hire and fire policy it was never familiar with. His style of management created a cold sense of fear. Things were changing, but changing too fast. I disapproved of many of his decisions. He was an angry man, and he lost his temper at the drop of a hat. But he knew he couldn't run the business without my help and support. I was never a YES man in my whole career, and that's what I preached to my team.

To give you an example, Ani once proposed to the board to launch our English newspaper, The Telegraph (TT), from Mumbai. I opposed the proposal tooth and nail, arguing that the venture would be unsustainable. After a lot of boardroom debate, the proposal was rejected. Ani was angry with me. Had the proposal been carried out, the company's financials would have been adversely affected.

The biggest lesson learned from Ani's stint was that one should not try to change the culture of any place or organisation overnight. Ani wanted to change the culture because he believed the ABP house culture needed change. But he tried to do it too fast. In the five years of his leadership, the company gained a lot but lost something precious. It was, and remains, imperative that ABP retain its true culture of caring and belonging while absorbing new values and processes.

3

Runway Revving

"Being good in business is the most fascinating kind of art … making money is art and working is art and good business is the best art."

– Andy Warhol

One of the most significant decisions in the history of the ABP group was its venture into news television. By 2003, STAR News had become a popular Hindi News channel in India. Existing regulations dictated that foreign holdings in Indian media companies had to be capped at 26%. The government demanded greater transparency in STAR's structure, although they were abiding by rules. They were asked to bring in an Indian media partner who would own at least 51% in the company. This was an opportunity that just presented itself to us.

Aveek Sarkar, the then Chief Editor, asked me one day whether it would be a good idea to bid. We didn't have deep pockets. My answer was: "This is a golden opportunity. We should not miss it. We shall find out ways to finance the venture." The rest is history. The Murdochs, fabled owners of the STAR ventures at the time, evaluated all leading Indian media companies, and most of them were interested. Aveek Sarkar flew to London and made a presentation to the Murdochs.

We had made our bid with two major advantages. We ran a successful joint venture in India with Penguin, UK. We were also on the verge of launching The Financial Times (FT) in India through a joint venture with Pearson. In fact, a number of FT journalists were sitting in our Delhi Bureau and writing stories regularly for Business Standard, our financial daily. Unfortunately, the FT venture did not come through because of red tape and bureaucracy, but that's a different story.

Despite our already expanding international media footprints, though, breaking into television wasn't easy. It took Arup Sarkar to convince Murdoch to seal the deal with us.

The final negotiations were to happen in India. The venue was the Star India offices in Mumbai. As James Murdoch led Aveek and Arup Sarkar into the negotiating room, I waited outside with Ani. I was so tense that I could hear the constant throbbing of my heart. I had assured Arup Sarkar not to worry about the financing. Arup Sarkar solely led the negotiations and came out beaming with the deal done. That was September 2003.

Hectic activity followed. I remember spending sleepless nights in the offices of investment bankers and top-flight lawyers, trying to get the financing and paperwork just right. On September 19 of that year, ABP formally acquired a 74% stake in STAR News. I had an early morning flight back to Delhi; I looked out the window of my plane seat and saw the sun lifting up, and the thought came to me that a truly new dawn had emerged upon the ABP group.

Mr. Aveek Sarkar is signing the agreement with Star

Celebration after signing of the agreement

The author is handing over the cheque to the Star representative

The author (on extreme left) is signing the agreement with Star

Aveek Sarkar became the Chairman of the Board of the company called MCCS, which would broadcast the channel. Arup Sarkar, Ani, Avijit Deb (our long-associated Solicitor) and I joined the board along with two of Star's representatives. Peter Mukherjee was one of them. He was a broad-hearted man and knew TV sales, distribution and marketing like the back of his hand. He was an easy-going bachelor aged fifty. One day, after the board meeting, he told us he was in love and marrying a girl named Indrani. That marriage was to ruin his life, with their involvement in the sordid murder of Indrani's daughter from an earlier marriage.

* * *

News Television was an entirely new experience; we knew the business of news but not television news. Day after day, I learned the tricks of the trade. Uday Shankar was the Editor and CEO. He later left us to head Star India, the country's leading entertainment company with a bouquet of multiple successful language channels. He then diversified the company into sports and created Hotstar, the famous OTT app. They were acquired later by Disney. Uday recently retired from Disney to pursue something of his own. He remains a close confidant of the Murdochs.

We realised that we should keep our focus on language channels. Having a premium positioning would be our USP. The ABP brand stood for quality and trust in Bengal and word had spread across the nation. We decided that we needed to have a bouquet of language news channels. After owning a successful Hindi News channel, we launched Ananda in West Bengal, the geography where we command a 60% share in the print media. The channel was an overwhelming success from day one. We then launched a series of news channels: Majha from Maharashtra, which also became the No. 1 news channel in Marathi. Then, Asmita from Gujarat became number one within two years. We couldn't launch Sanjha from Punjab because of political reasons. But such was the demand from the Sikhs of Canada that we launched the digital version of Sanjha in Canada.

Allow me to tell you a bit here about how television news comes into your living rooms and bedrooms.

About what goes on while you sit or lie there, watching the news.

The editorial functions of a news television channel are divided into two components – Input and Output. The Input side is responsible for gathering the news, and the Output side processes the news and makes it ready for your viewing. The Input team consists of reporters and cameramen. Reporters are spread across the geography that the channel serves. The streams of events recorded by them are transmitted to the servers in the headquarters of the respective channels. External agencies like ANI, PTI, AP, etcetera are also sources of news and become part of what may be called the Input feed.

After receiving the Input feed, the assignment desk gets activated. This desk is in charge of verifying the news received and using editorial discretion to see if these are worthy of broadcasting. At the same time, the wheels of planning what will air tomorrow are also churning in some other editorial meeting, and where reports and camera teams should be deployed.

The news that gets uploaded for further processing is picked up by producers and their teams which decide what news should be covered in their individual shows. According to the news feed picked, a storyboard is written—this is about how the news shall be finally presented. Then, graphics, videos and voice over (VOs) are prepared. If any assisting video is required, it is taken from the channel's library. The VO is recorded in-house from the script prepared and is synched with the video and graphics that are to be displayed with it. This combined piece is called a package, and an hour's show generally has 3-4 such packages.

This package is then transferred to the PCR (Production Control Room). The package also contains the anchor links, which need to be shot in the studio with the anchors. This can either be done as a live shoot or can be pre-recorded. The package, along with the anchor links, is now ready to be broadcast. There are also other elements in a news piece that may need to be included live, like any interview or phone call that is arranged by the guest desk in the Input team. Such feeds are taken directly by the PCR and displayed. The PCR schedules these packages one after the other, keeping slots for the advertisements to run. The PCR controls when the package needs to finish to break into ads, when is a graphic template to be switched from one to another, when the show opener is to be played, when the anchor is to be taken alive after the break, etc. The feed once passed from PCR, goes to the MCR (Master Control Room) to be uploaded to the satellite. The MCR is the final authority that checks what is going to be broadcast on the face of the channel. All these processes are backed up by seamless resource support ensured by operations teams working relentlessly behind the cameras.

The next leg is the distribution. The feed that is passed from the MCR is uploaded on the satellite and downloaded to the dish antennas of various distributors through a process called Uplink via the dish antennas placed at the headquarters. The distributors or the Distribution Platform Operators are responsible for transmitting the feeds to each household in the country either through another Uplink and downlink in the case of DTH operators or the cable networks run by the local distributors. The efficiency of the distribution function is determined by the distribution reach that the channel is able to garner in the geography it serves.

The bridge between sales securing advertisements and the PCR running them is the traffic department. This team consolidates all the ad commitments made by the sales team and ensures that they are run on the channel. They schedule all the ads in accordance with the respective Release Orders (ROs) and line up the break sequence. They coordinate with the Output team to ensure efficient utilisation of all ad inventory and execution of the sales contracts.

As you watch a news channel comfortably in your living room, all of the above activities are churning behind your screen 24/7, 365 days a year.

In 2005, Ani's five-year term ended, and he left, leaving behind a series of significant initiatives he pioneered. However, ABP was culturally battered.

The board decided to bring in another veteran who understood the ethos of ABP. Pramath Sinha's name was suggested. He was from McKinsey and was the lead consultant at ABP when we retained them twice. I was also called for an interview by the board, being a homegrown professional. Pramath was selected, and he joined as Managing Director & CEO in January 2006.

In May 2006, I became a member of the board, and my designation changed to Executive Director and COO. I had been placed on a huge learning curve. Many times, I was hauled up by Dr. Ashok Ganguly, who had earlier been Chairman of the Hindustan Lever Board; he was a man with exacting standards who would brook no compromise. I learned from my mistakes and quickly gained the confidence that I, too, have the ability to rub shoulders with those luminaries marching ahead of me in the ranks. So what if I didn't have an Ivy League stamp on my academic records? Later, during my term as the Managing Director, they bestowed tons of praise upon me for my performance year after year.

Pramath was a good friend of mine, and he, too, called me Purki. He started to rebuild the organisation. But he made some blunders. He recruited a group of people he knew and trusted and put them in charge of important functions like Finance, marketing, Strategy, and printing, violating the then-existing hierarchy. They worked as a parallel group and became Pramath's own think tank, so to speak. Pramath lost the trust and confidence of the official functional heads, each of them being homegrown. Often, the two groups would clash and quarrel; often, I had to mediate.

Pramath's second blunder was to increase the valuation of ABP and make it public. In this process, he brought in multiple investment proposals which were vetoed by me as the finance head. For example, one proposal was to start a free newspaper across India in partnership with the Dutch partner Metro. You might remember the English edition of *Metro* strewn all over the London tube and the stations. They claimed it to be a big success. But where are they now? The very idea of a free newspaper was eventually rejected globally. We at ABP didn't have the kind of deep pockets to fund such an expensive experiment.

Our relationship turned bitter over time as I didn't support his dreams. I couldn't believe that Pramath, a perfectly reasonable person as a consultant, could transform so much after taking the leadership role. His relationship with the promoters also deteriorated. In 2007, he resigned, and so did all his new recruits.

The Board had by now seen enough of the two outsiders brought in as CEOs after homegrown Shobha's tenure came to a close. I was supposed to retire in September 2007, after turning sixty. In August 2007, I was promoted to CEO. I still remember as Arup Sarkar guided me to my chair in the huge room, he congratulated me and told me, "Purki, you are wearing a Crown of Thorns from today. I am sure you will succeed and not let me down." I lived up to that until my last day at work in ABP. I led this beloved organisation for the next 14 years, and on 31st March 2021, I retired from my executive role after serving for 42 years—a contented man in every respect. I left the organisation in excellent shape and in the hands of the able team I had so carefully picked and nurtured. I am sure they would lead the company to dizzier heights.

* * *

After a successful first year, the board promoted me as the Managing Director & CEO. Those last fourteen years at the top were the most difficult I had to go through in my corporate life. Lehman Brothers went bankrupt, sending financial shockwaves across the globe. The launch of the iPhone and Android phones hastened massive digital penetration. Google and Facebook became giants overnight and our biggest competitors. The future of newspapers started to look gloomy with millennials consuming news from digital media, and social media threatened the content of legacy newspapers. The growth of advertising in newspapers, and to some degree in news television too, started declining. The Indian economy, which had been on an unprecedented upward trajectory, began to slow down. COVID-19 came like the final blow.

As circulation and advertising growth started declining, Indian newspapers began gaining shares from competitors. This led to a cover price war from which we could never recover. Newspapers in India are sold at a price between two to eight US cents. Most newspapers didn't raise the cover price for decades; almost 80 to 90% of revenue came from advertising. Advertisement revenue growth had fallen from high double digits a decade ago to low single digits.

ABP is the only truly diversified media house today. Most others have all their eggs in the newspaper basket. We had the foresight to diversify into TV in 2003 and into FM Radio in 2007.

As our circulation numbers grew and advertisers wanted to publish all advertisements in colour, we felt the need for a large press. In 2008, we started negotiating with Wifag of Switzerland. Their presses were the gold standard of printing. It was logical that their price was much higher than their competitors. They had barely any footprint in Asia. I led the negotiations, and finally, they agreed to a deal at an unbelievable price. Wifag's press is a gem, running at 82,000 copies per hour. Its high levels of automation deliver perfect colour reproductions. It needs only a handful of people to operate. The press line was installed in 2009 in a brand-new facility 50 km away from our office. Today, twelve years after its installation, it is churning out newspapers of the highest quality night after night. Both our newspapers continue to remain among the top three best printed newspapers from Asia, according to the research of the World Association of Newspapers and Newspaper Publishers (WAN-IFRA). We have also been a member of their Colour Quality Club continuously for the past 20 years for excellence in printing. This record made us a member of their prestigious Star Club.

My superiors often used to remark upon my negotiating skills. Shobha used to call me the 40% man. Negotiation is an art. You must know when to press a point when to allow a little leeway. Many negotiations fail because the greed for a better bargain is taken too far or because the fear of losing out makes you yield too much. A good negotiation is to tread along a thin line, a thing of delicacy and dexterity. You need to know when to hold back when to strike. My advice to young aspiring managers would be to practice this art carefully.

* * *

Among the first things I realised as I took over charge was that we did not know our customers. Our advertising sales staff spent most of their time with the media buying teams of the Advertising Agencies. At the end of the day, they carried the Release Orders (the document that authorises a publisher to print the advertisement). I didn't know sales and marketing at all. But the fact startled me.

I began my visits to the large advertisers, mostly in Mumbai, Delhi, and Bangalore. I was an unknown quantity to them. I started understanding their problems and the help they needed from us to market their products and services. The regional sales heads accompanied me to these meetings. We started offering marketing solutions. They were mostly jointly prepared. They started getting results, and their sales improved.

My customer visits increased to five to six advertisers a month. I remember meeting up to six advertisers a day, often crisscrossing the city. This was noticed by the media buyers, and my team often told me that the Ad agencies were getting annoyed by my visits. This made me more adamant. I believed that a publisher had every right to meet the advertisers who spend the money. I was the only CEO trotting around the country with my team. We and the advertisers often brought in the media buyers too at the table. Soon, I became a popular name. I was on first-name terms with the honchos of large ad agencies and advertisers. The backroom finance person in me was changing fast.

EBITDA to Revenue percentage touched an all-time high in 2010-11.

In 2012, we started negotiating with Star India to buy their 26% stake. By then, Uday Shankar had left us and joined Star India as CEO. The Murdochs were not interested in continuing with the news television business in India with a minority holding. I recall in April 2012, I was on vacation in New Zealand with my wife. One evening, I got a call from our lawyer that Star India wanted to close the deal quickly. The next morning, we were on a flight to India, cutting short the picturesque South Island tour. I hope someday we will visit again and complete our unfinished tour.

Uday and I had a number of meetings. Finally, the deal was closed on a humid October day in Mumbai. ABP became the 100% owner of the news television business. Within a couple of months, STAR News was rebranded as ABP News, and the rebranding became a campaign announcement across all major Indian media houses and platforms. It was an overwhelming success. ABP had transformed into a national media brand.

* * *

In April 2013, Atideb Sarkar, the younger son of Arup Sarkar, joined us. I shall never forget the request Arup Sarkar made of me upon Atideb's arrival. He told me not to treat him as a shareholder but as a fellow professional manager who was to be groomed as his successor. He wanted Atideb to learn the nitty-gritty of the business as he himself had learned it when he had joined the company's operations; he was barely 17 years old then.

Atideb had a Master's in Economics from the University College of London; he had graduated from Warwick University in England. He interned as a journalist at *The Financial Times* in London. He came back in 2010 and joined the news desk of *The Telegraph.*

From day one of his stint on the managerial side, I asked Atideb to join the Executive Committee. I advised him to listen to others, try to understand the business without making any comments and shadow me around, watching and grasping what I did. He did exactly so.

A young boy of twenty-one had now grown to be a mature business leader. Atideb is innovative and has a clear strategic outlook. The current CEO, Dhruba Mukherjee, reports to him. In July 2021, Arup Sarkar stepped back and took on a new role as Nestor, and Atideb took over as the Chief Editor and Publisher. Atideb had begun to attend newsroom meetings almost a year before. Part of him is a very engaged and informed journalist who has the ability to talk about and analyse issues across the board, from economics to politics to sports.

He has been attending a programme at Harvard Business School on successfully running a family business and was coached for a year by a senior professor at Harvard. He is now trying to implement what he learned in the Company. On my day of retirement, one of the prime reasons I felt contented was that Atideb was fully ready to run his family business and that I had kept the promise I had made to Arup Sarkar. I could see how proud he was as a father to see his young son grow into leadership roles at such a young age.

* * *

By 2010, the Bennett Coleman group had become a monolith towering over all competition in the print media. They are published from all the metro cities of India. They started offering a combination advertising rate covering all these cities under a brand name maximiser. Since they dominated the Mumbai market, and later Bangalore, advertisers had no other option in these cities. What the maximiser did was to charge pretty high rates for these two cities and a very small additional amount for taking other cities. As a result, they started gaining a major share of the advertising revenue market.

I could see trouble looming on the horizon; the Bennett Coleman behemoth was approaching. They launched The *Times of India* (TOI) in Calcutta, followed by Chennai. But *The Telegraph* and *The Hindu* dominated the two respective markets. Fierce competition started between TOI and *The Hindustan Times* (HT) in Delhi. The TOI was on a rampage. We had to respond. An idea occurred to me. I realised that all three of us, not only dominated our respective cities but our entire hinterland. TOI operated only from the cities. The combined reach between the three of us would be far more than that of TOI. They were weak in Calcutta and in Chennai. I devised an advertising alliance between HT, *The Hindu*, and TT similar to the Star Alliance. I approached Rajiv Verma, the CEO of HT, and Balaji, the promoter CEO of *Hindu*, with the idea. Rajiv responded positively, but Balaji was hesitant. The initiative failed. The failure ignited me.

I started with new vigour to convince Balaji. I shuttled between Rajiv and Balaji for a few years. By then, *The Hindu* had begun to face tough competition from TOI.

At last in 2013, *One India* was born. In 2014, *The Hindu* recruited Rajeev Lochan from McKinsey as the CEO. It was easy to convince Rajeev of the benefits of the alliance I had in mind. With his consultant's bent of mind, he fully supported the initiative. We recruited a veteran advertising person from TOI to head the business.

Years passed. After a few initial hiccups, *One India* started to grow. Around the same time, changes happened at the top in HT and *The Hindu*. L.V. Navneet, an old hand in *The Hindu* who had moved to Indonesia, returned as CEO. Praveen Someshwar, a PepsiCo veteran, joined as the CEO of HT. *One India* gained momentum. The growth in advertisements exceeded the market growth year after year. A new team was formed by pooling our individual resources. We followed up strong marketing campaigns with published readership data. Our message to the advertiser was: *One India* offers India on a platter with a formidable reach, much better than the competition. We strengthened the alliance further by adding our strong language newspapers. The *One India* bouquet became a success story.

From interactions with advertisers, I began to realise that they needed something more than plain vanilla advertising. Based on their inputs, we started a page in the newspaper branded "Patabahar", meaning a beautiful page. It was the beginning of Branded Content in the newspaper. To give an example, the content could be on weekend destinations written by our experienced editorial team. There was genuine reader interest in such subjects. At the bottom of the page, the automobile brand of the advertiser was subtly displayed. Readers could relate the brand to the destinations. This made a huge impact on advertisers. The device became such a darling of FMCG brands that they didn't mind paying a much higher price for space.

The demand from advertisers grew. They were now hungry for 360-degree brand solutions to address their focused targets; plain vanilla advertising was losing shine. My team member from that time, Aritra Sarkar, came up with a brilliant idea. He suggested we form a team to address this and capture the opportunity. He started a new department in 2011 and named it ABP One. Realising the growth in demand, we recruited copywriters, high-calibre sales and marketing cadres, and foot soldiers who could execute plans on the ground. ABP One was almost like an in-house ad agency that provided single-window services to clients on a turnkey basis. From understanding advertisers' targets and concerns to conceptualisation to execution, every detail was handled by this team.

After a few years, Aritra moved on. The leadership of the team changed. But the business continued to multiply. The list of our advertiser clients grew by leaps and bounds. Let me give you an example of how it worked. Cadbury wanted their chocolates to become a regular household purchase in Bengal. The state is famous for its delicious sweets made of cottage cheese. There is a sweet shop on almost every street corner. Bengalis prefer their homegrown brands and varieties of sweets to any other in the world; in fact, they are proud and zealous about their sweets and treat them as an intrinsic part of their culture.

It came as no great surprise that Cadbury was having trouble penetrating the Bengal market with its products. Bengal is no stranger to chocolates, but they had not become part of its quotidian mass culture or habit; chocolates were something you gave away or got on birthdays, that's all. Cadbury was at a loss on how it could bring a quantum change to how Bengalis viewed chocolates.

The idea our ABP One team came up with was an "election". The media agency of Mondelez India was Madison India. They lent us complete support and a free hand to work on the campaign through market insights. We approached some renowned Calcutta sweet shops to mix Cadbury Diary Milk with their cottage cheese and create a new brand of sweets. The names of the sweets were decided by them. We then launched a massive election-like campaign to vote for the preferred sweet shop of individuals. We picked out celebrities to endorse individual shops or chains. Over the next few weeks, these celebrities moved around Calcutta in open jeeps, mimicking election propaganda for their endorsed shops. We used Print, TV, Radio, and Outdoors to amplify the campaign, just as political parties do at election time. On the scheduled "election day," consumers were asked to vote for their preferred shop through their mobile phones. We received more than a million votes. We then organised an on-ground award event with the celebrities. The results were announced, and awards given. A mass hysteria-like storm engulfed the city for weeks. The result: Cadbury Dairy Milk grew ahead of other markets. Their market share increased for the same period over last year. A team flew in from their Singapore offices to congratulate us. Cadbury sweets became a regular shelf item in Bengal's sweet shops, and for the first time, the brand became a regular household buy. The ABP and Madison teams reaped a rich harvest of awards. In the first year, we won the Emvies and Abby Awards and went on to win many awards in the subsequent years. This became a continuous stream of new revenue for ABP. But our biggest gain was a satisfied customer for more than a decade.

Such examples are Galore and ABP One today is a resounding success and an established and appreciated brand in India. The list of advertisers includes Unilever, P&G, Coca-Cola India, PepsiCo, Kellogg's, Samsung,

Britannia, Colgate, GSK, Reckitt, Zydus, Airtel, Tanishq, Mahindra, and Future Group, among many others.

After the advertising team started regular interactions with advertisers, I turned my attention to our readers. Here, too, I discovered that our team interactions were only with agents, not with those who directly consumed our bouquet of products.

You must understand a little about how newspapers are distributed in India. This is how the supply chain works:

Once newspapers have rolled off the press, copies are transported by rail, air and road. Distribution by road is handled by our own or rented delivery trucks. There is a network of agents across the geography who receive these consignments and distribute them through a large group of hawkers. Hawkers collect newspapers from agents of all newspapers and deliver them to the readers' homes. The agents do not own the hawker network. In many cases, the same agent is retained by multiple newspapers, while some of them are unique to a particular newspaper. The agents earn a commission in the range of 25% to 40% of the cover price in different regions of India. The agents pay a portion of the commission earned to the hawkers. At the end of the month, publishers send invoices to the agents. They pay the publishers by the end of next month.

Many of the agents own other businesses, and they were not seriously or necessarily pursuing the growth of the newspaper business. Some are merely happy with their earnings and don't want to exert more to push the business. They are mostly illiterate folks and merely carrying on the family business of newspaper distribution. Most of the interactions of our sales staff with them were about their multiple grievances—newspaper arriving late, or the quality of content, or the competitor paying them more. In a nutshell, there was no accountability, and these sales calls ended in futile conversations. The blame for underperformance was always passed on to the hawkers whom we barely even knew and upon whom we had no control.

This was tolerable while the going was easy. But with the turn of the century, competition became aggressive. Publishers entered other publishers' geographies with the intention of grabbing their share of the circulation, the market and revenues. July 2002 marked the beginning of the Cover Price war in the Indian newspaper industry. It began in Delhi, and it was triggered by the TOI. They were the undisputed leaders in Mumbai, and so was HT in Delhi, with TOI a distant No. 2. The weekly package of HT was Rs 14.50 and that of TOI Rs. 12.90. In spite of a higher price, HT was, by far, the dominant newspaper of Delhi.

In July 2002, TOI reduced its weekly price pack to Rs 11 with a cover price of Rs 1.50 on some days. HT followed with a reduction to Rs 11.75 with Rs 1.50 on weekdays. In the next half-yearly Circulation Audit by the Audit Bureau of Circulation, TOI numbers went up from 3,90,000 to half a million, while HT grew from 4,90,000 to 5,50,000. The war raged on. Indian publishers discovered the benefits of price reduction. Almost all major publications started to follow suit in a bid to boost their market share. As a result, the market, too, began to grow. Indian publishers could never recover from this illness; the price wars still continue.

Before 2002, publishers used to increase the cover price every year. But since the day TOI began to reduce prices in order to undercut the competition, price increases have been few and far between. As a result, the ratio of advertisement and circulation revenue got completely skewed. It changed from 60:40 to 90:10; that is how ridiculous the ratio is today. This made all of us dependent only on advertisement revenue and thus became vulnerable to ups and downs in the larger economy.

And as the growth of advertising expenditure in print came down sharply, the business model became almost unsustainable.

The next move by TOI was the launch of subscription schemes. If a subscriber paid for six months in advance, the price dipped to Re one. Home delivery of newspapers continued through the same supply chain. But the agents were up in arms since their incomes fell sharply. They used to be paid a commission based on the printed cover price, which was Rs 4 or more. Thus, a publisher often had to pay from their pocket instead of earning any revenue. The readers found it very lucrative because we have a thriving used paper market—what we call the "raddi" trade; they got their returns, happily trading their newspaper stocks into the flourishing "raddi" trade. In fact, ghost readers appeared who started buying newspapers to sell as "raddi."

At the same time, though, newspaper publishers had to build and maintain an elaborate infrastructure to monitor subscriptions, keep an eye on renewals and push for new acquisitions. Large call centres were set up backed up by expensive Customer Relations Management (CRM) software. The cost of managing subscriptions ran high, and there were hardly any real revenues coming in. But circulation numbers continued to grow because of the undercutting of cover prices. Soon, advertisers started losing confidence in these ABC audited numbers. No one knew what was genuine and what was fake. Readership became the principal yardstick for measurement.

I took over as the CEO in the midst of these tectonic shifts in the trajectory of the newspaper industry. The TOI's price brinkmanship had demonstrated to the entire industry that it had become a cut-throat business, no place for the faint-hearted. As the competition grew, we started setting higher and higher targets for our sales force. The agents were not prepared to strive seriously for newer, higher targets. In order to achieve their targets, the agents were supplied more copies than they demanded. Most of these copies remained unsold, and the agents didn't pay for them. The outstandings started to mount. The mess was piling up, just like the unsold copies, an apt metaphor for the crisis we were in.

The need for intervention was urgent and desperate. That was the beginning of our relationship with the hawkers and readers. We created a database of hawkers, and we more or less knew, by then, which households they supplied our newspapers to. We started offering incentives to the hawkers, keeping a close eye on efforts to cannibalise them by the competition.

Alongside this, I started travelling across towns and villages of the state to meet the readers. These reader meets were pre-organised. Our reporters covering that region often accompanied me and the sales staff. Often, the news editor from Calcutta joined us. We used to meet at the local schools or town halls. The readers were asked to give us their honest feedback about the content of our newspaper with respect to our competition. We wanted genuine feedback, and this was an exercise to find out directly from our readers on what was required. We had not gone out looking for praise; we wanted criticism; we were looking for the readers' analysis of what we may be missing out on editorially. Those interactions became gold mines of data for the editorial team. Many of the suggestions and inputs we picked up on these field visits were incorporated into creating our editorial content. And, of course, the forays helped us plug holes in distribution and circulation.

We realised that the time had arrived for micro-news coverage for a newspaper that readers in the smallest unit areas could call their very own. In 2017, we launched a local newspaper for one of the districts as a pilot project. It was a newspaper with the same masthead distributed together with the main newspaper at no additional price. This new newspaper (Paper within Paper or PWP as we called it) covered everything local. From politics to sports to culture to the local issues and problems—everything found a place in this. Even the front page didn't carry any national or state issues. That resonated hugely with the readers, and they instantly saw in the PWP experiment an echo of their own concerns and interests. They embraced it with gusto.

Sales began to grow. Reader feedback was extremely encouraging. Within a year, we launched a PWP for each district in Bengal. The core lesson learned was that the customer is king. I wondered why we had left ourselves in such complete darkness—and at the mercy of uninterested and often mercenary agents—all these years. The solution was simple—reach out to the consumer of your product directly. Nothing stood in the way. We merely needed to cover that distance. Our go-local policy and the consequent PWP ventures achieved that. The Circulation Team was renamed Audience Development & Sales. Our newspaper marketing campaign tagline was changed to "Reader first". We knew we had got the tone of it just right.

4

Headwinds

"There can't be a crisis next week. My schedule is already full."

– Henry Kissinger

In November 2016, the Narendra Modi government demonetised key currency denominations overnight. It was a thunderbolt announcement. It sent shock waves across the country, such waves that would continue to shake and wreck for months to come, even years. Historically, a fairly large volume of business transactions was conducted in cash. That business was suddenly guillotined. A small window was provided to deposit old currency back in the banks. ATMs were not configured to churn out the new currency being minted. The nation was flung into chaos. From the smallest family unit to the biggest houses of business and industry, the blow was stunning; recovery was never going to be easy or swift.

Then came July 2017 and the Goods and Services Tax (GST) proposals—a single but complex tax regime to be implemented throughout the country. The decision was well thought out, and it would benefit the economy in the long run. However, the rollout of taxation changes on such a scale was far too rapid not to disrupt businesses.

Both the above decisions adversely affected the Indian economy. The GDP growth of India declined from 8% in 2015-16 to 7% in 2016-17, 6% in 2017-18 and 4% in 2018-19. I am quoting the reliable Macrotrends.net. And as our economy started slowing down, it took a heavy toll on the media industry.

Every industry started reducing costs to counter the fall in revenues. Advertising and promotional budgets were the first to be chopped. Advertisers diverted significant spending to digital media. It was far less expensive than print, and it had begun to provide a response because of how technology was changing the nature of news consumption. The Indian newspaper industry, already under pressure of falling reader demand, was the worst to suffer.

Our Advertisement revenues declined by 28% from 2015-16 to 2019-20. However, we didn't lose any market share as the whole pie collapsed. But that was no consolation. Believe me, those were the most challenging years of my career. But then, as I have mentioned earlier in my narrative, challenges have a way of coaxing the best out of me.

* * *

In mid-2015, at one of the monthly meetings of the ABP Executive Committee, I advised the Leadership Team that it was high time to look at our business model anew; unless we did that and responded to the new challenges in radical ways, we would get into trouble.

With the rapid advancement of technology, consumer behaviour was changing fast. By 2015, India had become the third country after China and the US with 250 million smartphone users (Source ICEA, KPMG, Statista). The young generation prefers to read the news on their smartphones. You had to be blind not to see the emerging trends of news consumption.

New digital technology-based companies became our competitors, and they were taking away large shares of our classified business. Newspapers were no longer the preferred destination for buying and selling automobiles and real estate. Our strong classified matchmaking business also started losing shares to these new kids on the block.

The display advertising business has not been affected so far. But American and European newspapers were losing revenues fast to newly-imagined and new technology platforms, mainly Google and Facebook, whose approach and intent were very aggressive. The Indian media industry was behaving like an ostrich, expecting that we would remain a secure island because of poor connectivity, paucity of news in the digital format and strong newspaper reading habits. We were wrong; the ground was fast shifting, and we would soon be shaky on our feet.

We had acquired none of the advantages of new technology platforms, and we remained burdened with the overheads of old trade practices and mores. For a start, our cost base was rather high compared to the kind of revenues we were able to generate for ourselves. Our revenues were not broad-based—circulation revenue remained stagnant due to the cut-throat competition between newspapers.

Classified advertisement revenues were dwindling. Display advertising will definitely follow the Western trend soon.

These were warning signs glaring at us. It was not possible any longer to bury our heads in the sand or to look away. The challenge had to be confronted and surmounted. We quickly set about devising a plan of action.

* * *

In order to retain our readers and create new revenue streams, we needed to embrace new digital technology. Digital content had to be created, and a business model readied so that we did not lose out.

We needed to build our own digital matchmaking business, which was growing and lucrative. This had to be done for two reasons—to arrest the fall in market share and to create another revenue stream. We also had to figure out ways of innovating and strengthening display advertising methods to specially tailor them to advertisers' requirements.

On the inside, we needed to re-examine costs in a comprehensive and dispassionate fashion. We could not afford to be flabby; every penny invested needed to bring returns, and we needed to be a sinewy financial outfit. Every element of costs and expenditure needed to be looked at, and we needed to ask ourselves, what if this cost is eliminated? There would be no holy cows in this process; we needed to be ruthless in order to survive the new challenges the market and technology were constantly throwing at us.

This Plan was presented to the board. The board, seized by the crisis and the urgency to amend our outmoded and, very often, extravagant ways, gave the green signal.

We retained the Boston Consulting Group (BCG) as our partner to chart our future digital business strategy. A cost optimisation team was quickly assembled from different brands and functions. They were given the authority to scrutinise every process and activity and ask the owner of the activity what if that activity was eliminated or merged with another function. They used Activity Value Analysis methods followed by McKinsey.

Our advertising teams were asked to find out the problems and requirements of advertisers and offer fresh solutions. The ABP One team helped the sales teams in assessing new emerging issues and providing solutions. Advertisers wanted better returns on investment on what they spent on advertising; their interest in plain vanilla advertising was waning.

Over a month or a little more, we visited the newsrooms of leading newspapers in the United States and the UK to explore their journey towards converting traditional print material to digital content. We received valuable feedback from their CEOs and Editors. Most of them said that they were at the same level of digitisation as us five years ago. But they had to put themselves through a massive transformation because of the sheer force of changing technology, consumer behaviour and the business needs of the market.

In a traditional newsroom like ours, news stories and photographs are received on servers from news agencies like PTI, Reuters, AP and AFP, from our reporters in the field, and from our news bureaus in Delhi, Mumbai and other major cities. The newsroom comes alive late afternoon and chugs like an engine till the wee hours when the newspaper has been put to bed. A team of sub-editors constantly monitors breaking news, downloads copy from the servers, prioritises news, edits copy, and gives hierarchy to content. Stories are laid out on assigned pages according to how the editors assess their importance. Alongside, advertisements are assigned to their respective locations on respective pages. After the newspaper is ready, generally in the late evening, it is released for printing and for the digital team.

The publishers we visited had integrated their newsrooms, and the same team would handle content for print, desktop and mobile consumption. Newsrooms abroad had begun to operate 24x7. Breaking news would first be delivered to mobiles, followed by desktops. And as the day progressed and content changed or expanded, the news needed to be updated. Huge screens in newsrooms constantly displayed stories that readers liked or didn't. Accordingly, the most liked stories were given preference and disliked stories were either relegated or taken off. Everything was technology and data-driven. In fact, the last to go to bed were the stories for newspapers, which had been refined during the day by reader preference. As a result, newspapers carried the day's most liked stories.

A remarkable transformation was taking place in newsrooms across the world on how news was served out and what its hierarchy would be. There was general agreement in the bigger management and editorial rooms that the biggest hindrance to change was coming from the culture of journalism and news organisations. As the saying goes, culture eats strategy for breakfast. Seasoned journalists, set in their ways and persuaded of their wisdom, could not accept the new rite of young techies and data scientists deciding what news was fit to print and what was not, what should get priority over what. The truth was they were only helping journalists become more intimate with reader preferences; at the end of the day, it was the editor, or teams of editors, who had the final say in what the hierarchy of content was.

Our visits to Western newsrooms were eye-openers. We came back and decided to invest in a brand-new digital content business; it would be called ABP Digital. A large team was recruited for product, content, technology, advertising, research and human resources. It was decided that print journalists would share content so that we do not create a duplicate set of reporters and sub-editors. The structure was like a start-up dovetailed into the larger structure of the legacy organisation. HR policies were liberalised for this young team. Many of the learnings from our trip were implemented.

We decided to merge both newsrooms in the future. A new journey started, and our page views and unique visitor numbers increased substantially.

At the same time, we launched ABP Weddings. We recruited a senior person from the leading matchmaking company to whom we were losing classified revenue share. The purpose was two-fold. Firstly, to arrest the fall in revenue and reverse the slide. Secondly, we want to grab a greater share of the market from our chief competitor. Instead of being defenders in the matrimonial ad market, we became the aggressor. The target set for the team was to become the leader and the most preferred digital matchmaking destination for Bengalis worldwide within three years.

Its success was such that ABP Weddings was spun out as a separate company in 2019. It is now the market leader in Bengali by far. Meanwhile, we launched a Marathi matchmaking business from Mumbai.

In 2019, another new venture began. It was named Admissiontree. School admissions in India are an issue of huge pain and strain for parents; the race to get their wards admitted to a good school and provide them with a solid educational platform can often drive them crazy. They have to stand in long queues at the schools to secure admission forms, and the agony needs to be repeated during submission. And yet, anxieties remain over whether their child will get in.

We offered an online digital solution to schools. The forms could be downloaded and uploaded online by the parents. We will send the uploaded forms to the respective schools. It would eliminate the huge administrative effort schools undertake every year during admissions. Parents, on the other hand, would save time standing in queues at multiple schools. We would charge the schools a fee for this service.

The idea clicked. By 2021, two hundred schools were enlisted at Admissiontree, and 40,000 admission forms were processed. We are now in the process of planning to launch similar services in other Indian cities, too.

The cost optimisation team was successful in bringing down expenditure substantially. We continued this process for future years. Our cost base went down by 12% between the financial years 2014-15 and 2017-18.

The above included manpower optimisation, too. Employee strength was substantially reduced during this period. But the whole process was handled with empathy. The following measures were taken :

1. We offered handsome compensation.

2. We retained a renowned recruitment and career counselling agency to help provide alternative job opportunities.

3. We retained an experienced psychological counsellor to handle any trauma that resulted from the process among staff members.

4. A representative from a leading bank helped with investment opportunities for severance packages and financial compensation being received by those asked to part ways. We provided separate closed chambers at our office for them to operate.

Rationalising staff strength is never easy; very often, it can be a painful and emotionally taxing exercise. But in the way we undertook the exercise and through the design of our compensation packages, we saw to it that there was a happy feeling among those leaving. The exercise also strengthened the belief among employees that ABP cares.

Meanwhile, the advertising team mastered the art of solution selling. For a few large FMCG companies, we offered to share the benefits achieved. For example, some deals were market share-linked. For every percentage increase in market share, our revenues grew exponentially. It was a win-win deal for both.

In the financial year 2017-18, the company delivered excellent financial results with the highest-ever EBITDA/Revenue percentage over the past seven years. During moments of such radical change, it is imperative that the communication down the line must be clear and transparent. Otherwise, it leads to panic, anxiety and rumour-mongering.

Keeping this in mind, Town Hall meetings were organised. In May-June every year, I travelled to all our major offices to address every employee. Executive Committee members travelled with me. The Town Hall meetings were branded MD's Review. I explained the company's performance for the year gone by and our plans for the coming years with no ambiguity. Future opportunities and challenges were explained. At the end of the session, employees were free to ask any questions to clear their doubts or offer suggestions. My team and I answered all their queries.

The lesson I have learned through my professional life is that a leader must tell the truth, even if it is bitter. It is never recommended to paint a rosy picture of the future when it is not. I have given honest feedback to my teams during their appraisal process, highlighting their strengths and weaknesses. Every time, I noticed that this helped them in trying to overcome their weaknesses.

In October 2017, I took a bold decision. It was kind of a gamble. I moved Suman Banerjee, the head of Audience Development & Sales, to lead our HR functions. Suman was a sincere person. He was eager to learn. He was trusted by all. He has gained extensive experience in circulation, marketing, and advertising. I was getting feedback that people were uncertain about their careers, the appraisal process was perceived to be not so transparent, and people were resorting to desperate methods to meet targets. The cheer among the employees was missing.

Suman knew nothing about HR. But my gut feeling was that he would do an excellent job in HR. He was nominated for a one-year postgraduate programme in HR Management at XLRI, one of the country's best HR management schools.

Suman's brief was simple and clear—bring cheer back to the ABP workplace and put a smile on the lips of every employee at the end of a hard day's work.

Suman did a wonderful job. Within three years, he transformed the mood of the organisation. He loved the new role, and I was so happy that my gamble had paid off.

* * *

As financials turned healthy, we became liberal in spending in the financial year 2018-19. Yearly increments and variable pay were much higher than in previous years.

ABP, by then, had turned into the most diversified company in the Indian media industry with newspapers, magazines, national and regional news television, FM Radio, digital matchmaking, digital school admissions, special events and conference platforms; we had taken the lead in most of them. Our revenues were spread among multiple baskets. Our news television business was generating a healthy topline and bottom line.

Two major media technology trends continued. By 2019, the number of smartphone users increased to 635 million, and secondly, advertising revenue for newspapers continued to decline. In the financial year 2019-20, ad revenues fell by a whopping 16%. Both these were major concerns in our risk matrix.

And just as we were trying to explore a new business model for newspapers to sustain in the changing consumer and advertiser behaviour, some ominous news started pouring in from Wuhan in China. It was December 2019.

5

Midair Jolt

"It's not the tragedies that kill us, it's the messes."

– Dorothy Parker

In September 2019, a stray thought struck me. Why should our employees travel to the workplace every day? They spent 2 to 4 hours every morning merely commuting to work and a similar amount of time getting back home, trudging through traffic, which can often be painfully slow and torturous. I thought it was such a waste of time and energy, and yet we never thought of it that way.

If, instead of spending wasteful time and expending energy on their daily two-way commute, employees could work from their homes, their productivity was likely to improve. That, I thought, would be on two counts—they would be spending more time at the job, and, at the same time, they would be able to have a more enriched time with their families and dear ones.

I sounded out my colleagues on the Executive Committee on the idea. Some of them objected vehemently. They thought it was a utopian idea and could never be implemented. But some of them were not averse; they, in fact, supported it.

Convinced with my idea and armed with support from my team, I took up the challenge and implemented it in our offices in the South and the West. To begin with—Bangalore, Chennai, Hyderabad, Pune and Ahmedabad were chosen as centres for the pilot work from home (WFH) project. These offices had far fewer employees than our Mumbai or Delhi offices. When the idea was broached with them, they were ecstatic.

A team was formed with HR, IT and finance personnel to implement it by December. The team faced many hurdles, and I was not surprised. Some were cultural, and some were typical examples of resistance to any form of change. But some problems were technical or logistical, too. The specialist team we had created weeded out the problems one by one. A rule book was created by HR, which was later expanded into our group's full-fledged WFH Policy.

In January, we advised all our employees in those offices to work from home. By March, we terminated all lease agreements on the office premises we had hired. The going was smooth. We saved a large chunk of costs, and, more importantly, the employees were happy—being spared the drudgery of the daily commute was a huge relief.

Of course, not everybody thought the way I and some others did; I am aware that WFH, as an idea, had its opponents. But that was a challenge I had undertaken because I was convinced that it was the way to go ahead.

And when a global health disaster struck in the form of COVID, the WFH notion suddenly began to suggest itself more strongly. With all the restrictions that came with

COVID—the sudden and complete lockdown to begin with—most folks were clueless about how to make a large organisation work. This we had equipped ourselves ahead, almost as if we had anticipated a time when working out of huge offices would become unfeasible. Even after close to two years of COVID restrictions, I am not sure how many organisations have been smart or swift enough to achieve an efficient 100 per cent WFH culture. For us, though, it was a cakewalk. We just replicated in Calcutta and other major centres what we had already done in the South and the West.

The Coronavirus was spreading very fast from Wuhan right across the globe. It was like a health emergency of a scale and depth that the modern world had not seen. By February, infections started being reported in India. But the cases were few. Soon, though, cases began to grow exponentially, and by March, the situation had turned quite alarming.

On the evening of 24th March, Prime Minister Narendra Modi ordered a complete nationwide lockdown for 21 days, a regime that would be extended in four phases till 31st. May. But it wasn't only India that had been hit. The world had come to a halt as never before. Countries sealed their borders, international transport operations ceased, and the movement of people of goods and services took a huge, unprecedented blow.

The shock of the manner and speed with which the Coronavirus struck was huge. Few were prepared to absorb the impact of it. Production and distribution of goods and services came to a standstill overnight. People became scared for their lives, and their livelihoods suffered. A large workforce lost their jobs. The news of pandemic deaths began to pour in from all sides. Rumour and panic spread like wildfire.

Newspaper distribution came to a standstill as hawkers were afraid to go out. Readers stopped buying newspapers for fear, very irrational, of course, that newspapers would get the virus into their homes. Advertisers stopped advertising, which came as no surprise. Supply chains had come to a grinding halt, and consumers had stopped buying. Who would advertise what in such circumstances?

We stared at a bleak future without any circulation or advertising revenues. Nobody had any idea how long this crisis was going to last and what its short, medium and long-term impact would be on the media industry.

I had never been confronted with such an enormous problem ever in my professional career. I realised it was a question of our survival and that we must act without any delay.

It was decided not to stop publishing newspapers and keep the distribution chain up and running. It was a tough decision, but a decision that had to be taken in the face of the heaviest odds. We are a newspaper concern. What are we to do without a newspaper to publish and distribute to our readers? That is our dharma; we resolved, single-mindedly, that we shall not abandon it, come what may.

We launched a campaign to inform the readers that our whole supply chain was untouched by human hands, and newspapers were delivered home by hawkers wearing gloves and masks. We distributed the gloves and masks themselves freely to our entire hawker network. This also went a long way in instilling confidence among hawkers and readers alike at a time when the dread of the pandemic was widespread.

The Covid awareness campaign

We made arrangements to keep our employees and their families safe. We advised all our employees to work from home. Only a skeletal editorial and production staff was picked up and dropped home by transport vehicles kitted out with the utmost health and safety protocols.

We embarked on a massive cost reduction drive and started implementing it within a week. Key aspects of this drive were :

1. Close down all offices across India except our headquarters. Terminate all the lease agreements.
2. Discontinue all unprofitable editions.
3. Reduce newspaper pages.
4. Reduce 30% of our staff strength with handsome compensation.
5. Initiate a voluntary salary reduction regime between 15% and 30% for employees above a certain salary threshold.
6. Stop taking new subscriptions and phase out the current subscription over one-year. Close down expensive backend subscription support.
7. Convert most ground events and conferences into a virtual format.
8. Reduce overhead expenses substantially.

These measures almost immediately yielded a 30% reduction in base costs and expenses. Most of the cost reductions would be perpetual in nature.

We prepared an interim budget anticipating a 40% fall in advertisement revenue and a financial break-even for the financial year 2020-21.

The HR department was advised to monitor every employee and their families with immediate medical care for anyone infected by the virus.

Having satisfied myself that these measures had been taken in earnest, I addressed employees in a Town Hall meeting. They were told that everything was under control and their lives and livelihoods had been protected. They should not panic and pay no heed to rumours. It gave me immense satisfaction that we saved the organisation from disaster and placed it on a sound footing and ready for the future.

At the end of the year, the fall in advertisement revenue was 50%, and we missed our break-even target by a narrow margin.

The credit goes to my EC team, who converted a big threat to our beloved and historic enterprise into an opportunity in four months. The company is now lean and healthy and ready to face any new challenges. This could not have been possible under normal circumstances. COVID made it possible.

6

Long Haul

"Man grows beyond his work, walks up the stairs of his concepts, emerges ahead of his accomplishments."

– John Steinbeck

By 2011, ABP was one of the largest media conglomerates in India. However, the brand was barely known outside India.

The two largest media associations in the world are WAN-IFRA and INMA. Between them, they produce 50,000 print and digital news publications. They are competing organisations. WAN-IFRA has a strong presence in Europe, Asia and Africa. Their prime objective is to uphold press freedom and innovate on sustainable business strategies. INMA has a strong base in the Americas, Europe and Australasia. INMA's strength lies in how it devises business strategy, especially with respect to marketing and the transformation to digital platforms.

In 2012, WAN-IFRA invited me to join their Supervisory Board. After that, I was elected by the board as Chairman of the Advisory Council to provide guidance and advice to the board. I was then nominated as Special Adviser to the Board President, Tomas Brunegard, the then-CEO of Schibsted. While I was chairing the meetings at WAN-IFRA and deciding on policies, I often recalled the conference I attended in Amsterdam in 1982, which I shall briefly refer to in the next chapter. I was a nervous young 35-year-old delivering his first address to a gathering of media veterans.

In 2017, I recommended that a small body be formed from within the WAN-IFRA Board to fast-track decision-making. The Supervisory Board was too large, with members from every country, and often, there were too many opinions on one issue for decisions to be taken quickly. The Executive Board was formed in 2018 with a maximum of eleven members. The Executive Board comprises the President, Vice President, Treasurer and eight other dynamic board members, mostly young. I still continue as a member of the Supervisory Board.

In June 2021, as I was writing this book, I was invited by the Executive Board to join the Nominating Committee. It is an eight-member Committee that formulates plans for succession for non-executive Directors and for the key executive roles of President, Vice President and Treasurer. It makes recommendations to the Supervisory Board concerning the re-appointment of the executive Directors at the conclusion of their terms and also identifies and recommends any new appointment to the Supervisory Board. It was an honour for me to be invited to this key Committee of WAN-IFRA.

In 2013, I was invited by INMA to join their board. I sought permission from the WAN-IFRA President, asking if they had any objection to me joining the board of a competing media association. The WAN-IFRA Board had full trust in my integrity; they agreed. When I joined the INMA Board, I became the only person in the world to represent both the INMA and WAN-IFRA Boards.

My term at INMA expired in 2017. However, the board elected me for another term, which expired in June 2021. I finally retired from the INMA Board on July 1, 2021.

During my tenure in both the associations, I addressed numerous global congresses, conferences and seminars. I made many friends across the world. I call most of the media CEOs by their first names. My name has been abbreviated to DD by most of them, and everyone in the global media community calls me by that name.

The ABP brand is now recognised globally. At my request, Espen Egil Hansen, INMA Board member and the then CEO and Editor of Aftenposten of Norway, joined the ABP Board as an invitee. He served the board for a few years.

Many INMA and WAN-IFRA Board members came down to ABP for consulting assignments over the years. We benefitted a lot from their insights and counsel as well. ABP joined their Global Awards Programmes and received gold, silver or bronze trophies every year. The award ceremonies were attended by 400 to 500 members every time. ABP was, by then, a familiar name across the world.

Ananda Bazar Patrika and *The Telegraph* won the "Best Printed Newspapers in Asia " trophies year after year.

My journey over 42 years is the story of the transformation of ABP from an easy-going regional newspaper house to a globally respected, diversified and ambitious national media conglomerate. It is also the story of my journey from the bleakness of small north-eastern towns to the top of the league in Calcutta.

We now operate like any other large multinational corporate house. We have a well-drawn-out organisation structure, a digitised, transparent and objective performance management system with targets aligned to a common goal, an effective succession planning procedure, a strong customer connection and the best global technology. The fundamental guiding force of this engine is the pursuit of excellence backed by a strong value system that lies at the core of the ABP ethos.

Author with the Star Performers of the Year

We respect gender neutrality. We are extremely sensitive to any kind of harassment of female employees. The Sexual Harassment Committee is headed by a senior female employee, with two well-known personalities who are non-employees. The Committee has four female and two male members. The Committee recommends the verdict of any investigation of harassment to the CEO. The final decision is taken by the CEO in consultation with the Committee. In many instances, we have terminated high-performing employees if proven guilty.

Having said what I just did about us being a professionally cut-out corporate house of the best international standards, I do miss a few things about the way we used to be. I miss, for instance, the individual connects with folks, possibly only in a much smaller, close-knit outfit. I miss some of those long chats over a spread of "muri" or puffed rice, which, I now realise, made for an excellent HR session. I miss some of the family excursions we took together on weekends or even extended drinking sessions; we could put away a lot of alcohol in our times; my colleagues these days are mostly teetotalers.

Change is not merely inevitable, it is essential. But it is equally true that there remains in the heart a residual romance of times gone by. Corporate life has become much more structured and formal, but in my opinion, a CEO must be able to connect with colleagues outside of their day-to-day work regimen to provide them the opportunity to relax and express their feelings. I believed in interacting as freely and as often with colleagues during retreats and off-site programmes or excursions. A degree of informality of exchange helps people get a better understanding of each other. In today's stressed working conditions and the constant worry to meet the targets, this relief is extremely important.

I remember one such occasion when I was out with our sales team in Jodhpur in Rajasthan.

We went out for a short camel ride in the desert, like a little adventure or an excursion. Riding a camel is an experience all its own; nothing quite matches it. It can be fun; it can be equally frightful. I have a photograph with me astride a camel and our then-regional manager of northern India behind me. He hugged me so hard and had such a frightened expression on his face; it makes me laugh to this day. It is one of those photographs, like a "Kodak moment."

Riding a Camel

On another occasion, we faced a sudden emergency. I accompanied the team on a tour of Penang Island in Malaysia. We were warned at the hotel that the sea was full of jellyfish and no one should venture into the waters. The alert was clearly communicated to the team. But one of our sales managers decided to wade in for a swim. He came up gasping, his face crimson. He had been stung by a deadly jellyfish. He was in extreme pain and in galloping respiratory distress. We immediately moved him to the nearest hospital. He was administered an anti-allergic injection; his wound was dressed. He recovered after a while, much to the relief of the whole team. The sting of a jellyfish can be fatal. However, we were saved that day. In the evening, we danced together, and he, too, joined.

I cannot omit mention in this memoir of my working life some people—or shall I say, personalities—who transformed the organisation in their very unique ways.

Apurba Sengupta, Head of Production, remained unfazed in any serious discussions about the imminent risks we are facing. He would have a smile on his face with no visible concern. He was named the Smiling Buddha.

Amitabha Datta, SBU head of the dailies, was scared of flying. One evening, both of us were flying from Chennai to Calcutta. We were sitting in the airport lounge. Amitabha repeatedly gazed at the overcast sky with dark clouds. He prodded me a number of times about the weather. But when he failed to fetch a response from me, he did something strange. He went to the Captain of the flight and advised him not to fly in such weather conditions. The Captain laughed it away and assured him a safe flight. All options closed, he went to the bar and consumed two bottles of beer. I had to wake him up as we landed in Calcutta; he had slept all the way.

Biswaroop Chakrabarty, Head of Purchases, was argumentative to the extreme. He would come to my office to help him pick between options. But he would have already made up his mind and would argue for hours to defend his choice. The meetings would remain inconclusive. Then, I decided that in any such case of a difference of opinion, I would order him to go for the option I deemed most suitable. It worked like magic. He happily executed my option. What he wanted was an order, not a dialogue.

I discovered after a long time that one of our Advertisement Managers, Ritesh Chakrabarty, was a sharpshooter and was issued a licence by the government to shoot rogue elephants. I called him one day to share his experiences. What he had to tell me was chilling. An elephant that kills humans unprovoked is generally declared rogue by the Forest Department. Once it is spotted, they use tranquiliser shots to temporarily immobilise it. The circumference of its feet, height, size of ears, length of tail, etc, are carefully recorded. The elephant is then transferred to a different forest, and its behaviour is strictly monitored. Sometimes, they use radio collars to track the elephant. If the elephant continues to kill, the Forest Department issues orders for the elephant to be neutralised or killed. The hunter and Forest Department hands enter the forest and track the rogue elephant. The hunter is accompanied by his assistant as a backup. The killing has to be face-to-face. The distance from which the elephant is shot varies from 45 ft to 120 ft. The only two vulnerable organs are the brain and the heart. The outer part of the brain is a hard shell. The heart is inside the joint of its front legs with the body. There is a cushion-like area just below the eyes where the trunk begins. The shot must enter this area to hit the brain. Ideally, it can be killed by one perfect shot to the brain. Ritesh uses a 0.458 Winchester Magnum Rifle. Once the shot is fired, the hunter cannot move till the elephant falls dead.

Once, Ritesh had to face an elephant from a distance of only 20 feet. He fired the first shot. The elephant dropped to the ground but immediately stood up and charged him from the front. He killed it with a second shot. He said it would be suicidal to turn back and run without firing the second shot. The hunter must hold his position till the elephant is killed.

Ritesh with a killed rogue elephant

When I asked him why he chose this dangerous profession, he said it was the sheer joy of hunting and the satisfaction of killing an animal which had gone rogue.

* * *

During my long years at ABP, one of my greatest successes was earning the love of my colleagues. At my farewell function, I could feel the palpably high emotions of people and how much they loved me. My biggest gift was a framed copy of the front page of *Anandabazar Patrika*, which was published on the day of my joining. It was signed by six people who directly reported to me, and they had written out a comment: "For us, the headline news was Dipankar Das Purkayastha joined ABP that Wednesday, beginning a journey that went on for 15218 days or 42 years."

I shall never forget this eternal bond that will bind me to them and the memories I shall have with them till my last day.

The Nest

*"One does not have to get anywhere in a marriage, it's
not a public conveyance."*

– Iris Murdoch

None of what I have said about my professional life and
successes would have been possible without the family
I have been so fortunate to have around me. My wife
Kamala is the axis around which our lives rotate; mine
does, at any rate. She is a source of constant inspiration
and encouragement. She is joy; she is fulfilment, and she
is, in many ways, the beginning and the end of things for
me. Whenever I felt drained out, Kamala was the one who
filled me with the energy to start all over again and move
forward. She believes in a simple lifestyle. Today, we live in
an apartment in an upmarket neighbourhood of Calcutta. It
is a simple two-bedroom apartment. She never allowed me
to move to a larger place that the CEO of a large corporate
group deserves. The apartment is not kept very tidy. Her
logic is: It's our home and not a five-star hotel. Let it be a
bit unkempt, as everything at our home is natural and not
artificial.

As my son Dipanjan—our only child—started going to
school, her life became completely centred around him. She

was his constant companion. Like my father, she made him believe in God. She taught him never to do anything wrong and to be kind to people. She taught him whatever she knew and believed in. She would carry his tiffin to the school, interact with the teachers, and keep track of his progress. In the evenings, she accompanied him to the private tutors' residence and waited for hours, often standing outside till his lessons were complete. It became my daily chore to pick them up late in the evening on my way home from the office.

He passed the Secondary board exams (Standard X) with pretty high marks in most of his subjects and got admitted to St. Xavier's College (my alma mater) in Standard XI.

He has been a smart and intelligent child. In 1982, I was invited by the CEO of IFRA (The Global Association of Newspapers) to deliver a talk at their annual conference in Amsterdam. That was my first trip abroad, and I took my family along. As I entered the conference hall, I was fairly nervous, looking at the profiles of my fellow speakers. They were veterans of large newspaper groups across Europe. I was dwarfed by their stature. My wife and son sat beside me in the hall. Eight-year-old Dipanjan was providing me with the courage I desperately needed at that moment. He was explaining to his mother about the gadgets on the table he had never seen before and how to switch between different languages as the presentations were translated. My turn came, and I realised I had done a fairly good job. The audience heard with rapt attention the story of how a fledgling regional newspaper from India operated and performed so well. We travelled across Europe and came back with lots of confidence.

After Dipanjan got admitted to St Xavier's College, my workload increased a lot. I realised that I was getting distanced from him. His world revolved around his mother. Many times, I couldn't understand their conversations. My son was enjoying his teenage years to the fullest. He was the best dancer in college; fellow students called him Jackson. He was a good singer, too. He grew up to be a handsome young boy. At that time, he was even dreaming of joining Bollywood.

My mother had retired by then and was living with us. I noticed that she was losing weight. She was suffering from chronic acidity. I made an appointment with a young gastroenterologist who was practising in the UK and just returned to Calcutta. His name is Kalyan Bose. Kalyan later became a good friend of mine. But that's a different story. Kalyan examined my mother and decided to perform an endoscopy the next day. That fateful day after the procedure, he called me aside and told me he was certain she had cancer of the oesophagus, a prognosis that was later confirmed. He advised immediate surgery. I was devastated; I went numb and cold. I can never forget the help ABP provided in taking her to Mumbai immediately and getting her operated. I shall remain grateful to the group forever for saving my mother's life. This is the culture of ABP I often talk about. I am yet to see a more benevolent employer. The employees knew that the big umbrella would protect them in their difficult times. By God's grace and the wizardry of the surgeon at Tata Memorial, Dr Praful Patel, my mother was completely cured after the surgery.

Dipanjan passed out of college the following year. We wanted him to be an engineer, possibly because I couldn't pursue it because I could not afford the finances required for an education at the IIT, Kharagpur.

He was selected at two renowned engineering institutions, one at the Jadavpur Engineering College in Calcutta and the other at the Regional Engineering College at Kurukshetra in Haryana (it is now called the National Institute of Technology). In spite of vehement objections from my wife and my son, I put my foot down. I realised that if he continued his higher studies in Calcutta, Dipanjan would remain a mama's boy. Kurukshetra was a National Engineering College with students and faculty from across the country. He needed exposure and familiarity with other parts of India and Indians from other cultures.

I remember the day he was admitted to Mechanical Engineering in Kurukshetra. The beautiful green campus was in the middle of farmlands all around. It was a typical north Indian village. The surroundings were idyllic; most vehicles moving around were tractors carrying crops or farm equipment. There were hardly any fancy food joints nearby, barring a few shanties serving roti, dal and vegetables. Non-vegetarian food was banned in Kurukshetra on religious grounds; this, after all, is the site of the mythical battle between the Pandavas and the Kauravas of Mahabharata.

As we entered the campus, my wife's voice started choking. We went to have lunch together at the students' canteen. The food served was rice, rajma and some vegetable curry.

Tears began to roll down Kamala's cheeks, and she could hardly eat anything. It was a sad evening that day when we bid goodbye to our son and left. My wife was cursing me, saying that I had given the biggest punishment to her by leaving her son in exile in an alien land. I tried in vain to stop her from weeping all the way back to Delhi. I felt guilty, but I was confident I had made the right decision for my son.

During my tours to Delhi, Dipanjan would join me and tell me about his joys and woes. We became friends, and we thoroughly enjoyed those four years. He used to come home during vacations. He went around to meet his old friends. I could feel Kamala's pain at getting away from her beloved son. She had put everything at stake to make him an ideal person. They were soul mates. It used to hurt me, too, as a father. But I got my best reward when, after many years, he told me: "Dad, the best decision of your life was to send me to Kurukshetra. That's what made me whatever I am today."

After passing out, Dipanjan got a number of job offers. He picked up an Indian company that made branded jeans. He moved to Mumbai. After a couple of years, he joined Godrej-GE, a joint venture that manufactured home appliances. He joined as a Service Engineer. My wife and I were happy because he was able to relocate to Calcutta. He got engrossed in the job and quickly got a raise. But I was a little worried for him; I saw in him a contentment that isn't always good in someone who wants to rise.

Author with his wife

Author with his wife

Two years went by. One day, I called him and told him that he needed to change his orbit. After four years on a couple of jobs, he needed to return to studies to enrich himself; I believed he should study Management. An engineer with a management degree would enhance his career prospects substantially. He listened carefully. He then took his

GMATs and got a few admission offers from colleges in the US. He asked whether I would be able to afford his studies in the US. I was not earning enough to support his studies in the US. Kamala told him bluntly that unless he got a scholarship, it would not be possible to support him. At that time, he proffered a strange proposal. He suggested that he would take a bank loan mortgaging our house. I was soft with him and pondered over it. Kamala was fuming. She told him in clear terms that however doting a mother she might be, she would never allow mortgaging our residence. If he was so eager to study in the US, he had to fend for himself. She also told him that we would give him the best education within our means. But after that, he should never expect his father to arrange a job for him or provide monetary support. He was taken aback by his mother's words.

Author with his wife

He started looking for the best Management schools in India. He prepared himself and appeared in CAT, the national exam for entry into management schools. He was selected at S.P.Jain School of Management in Mumbai, one of the top schools after the IIMs. I told him to go ahead and not to worry about financial support. A new chapter of his life had begun.

Now our meeting venue changed to Mumbai. On my tours to Mumbai, either I went to his campus, or he came to my hotel. We discussed work and studies and life on the campus like two adults, man to man. He was carrying a lot of homework back from his class: management case studies, backgrounders for presentations, and further reading from beyond the prescribed texts. He turned into a night owl. He used to go to bed often at four in the morning and be up by 7:30. He still continues this habit.

Author's wife and daughter-in-law

During one of those interactions, he told me that he was in love with a girl named Shipra. She was his classmate. She was a Marwari girl from Mumbai. As he was showering praises on her, I realised he was madly in love. I met her on my next visit. I liked her perspective on life and the simple way she carried herself. She was from an educated conservative family, not a typical party-hopping cosmopolitan type you can run into big glamour cities like Mumbai. After a while, Dipanjan asked me whether I would approve if they got married. Well, of course, I told him; both were elated to have my consent.

But the bigger task of convincing Kamala remained. I thought she wouldn't approve of a girl from a different community and reject the proposal outright. Instead, she advised her son to respect women and to be dedicated to her since they were going to get married. If someday before their marriage, he felt he didn't like her anymore, he should tell her upfront and without any delay. Kamala hadn't even met Shipra in person at that time.

In March 2002, both passed out of the Management School and started looking for jobs. Shipra's dad wanted my son to be settled before getting married, while Kamala insisted that they should get married immediately after Dipanjan got a job.

Dipanjan joined Patni Computers, a renowned IT company; they were setting up their Business Process Outsourcing (BPO) venture from scratch, so Dipanjan moved to Delhi. He married Shipra in February 2003. The wedding reception was arranged in Calcutta with full grandeur. The elite of

Calcutta and my friends and peers from all over India were invited. Celebrities were all around; it was a starry night for us. That evening, my thoughts went back to the frugal reception Kamala, and I was able to afford when we got married all those years ago; it seemed like a memory from another world.

Author's wife and grandson

Author, wife and grandson

By 2005, Dipanjan had helped propel the BPO business from scratch to 3500 persons, and he was asked to join Patni Computers Inc. in Cambridge, Massachusetts, to promote their US business. Shipra left her HR job in Delhi, and they moved to the US.

Author's grandsons

We were happy parents. We had never seen the fascinating New England fall. Dipanjan took us in his new Lexus GS for a drive on the Kancamagus highway. The fancy music system on the car's dashboard was playing my favourite songs. The trees all around were glowing in multiple hues, from brown to orange to crimson. The weather was awesome, with bright sunshine and azure skies. Some days in your life you can never forget. That day, being driven around by my son in the American fall was one of those days.

In March 2007, our first grandson Ishan was born at Brigham & Women's Hospital, one of the best medical facilities in the world. I was ecstatic about becoming a grandfather. Ishan's birth was not easy. Shipra developed pre-eclampsia. Dr. David Olson and his team almost gave her a second life. God is kind.

In 2008, they bought a lovely house in Framingham, a quiet and quaint suburb of Boston. Dipanjan's career graph was rising. He was made a partner in the firm as he had been able to expand their Financial Services business exponentially. Patni was acquired by iGate in 2011.

My second grandson, Imon, was born in 2010 at the same hospital under medical conditions similar to Shipra's. My two grandsons are true gifts of God.

In 2011, Dipanjan joined Tech Mahindra as Vice President and head of strategic global relationships.

Author's Wife and son

He negotiated a deal to work out of Calcutta. It may have been tough to return once the two boys had grown beyond a certain age. Shipra, too, was very keen to move back home; we were thrilled to be with our grandsons.

For the next three years, he led one of the largest deals in Tech Mahindra worth $1.5 billion. I was convinced that sending him to study away from home was the right decision.

Author's grandson

In 2014, he left the job at the peak of his career to set up his own start-up. He asked for my approval, which I quickly gave.

After a few failed ventures, Dipanjan co-founded hyperXchange, a Refurbished Electronic brand, and it is now one of the top two players in India.

They live in an apartment nearby. Ishan is now a handsome teenager, and Imon is a fun-loving 11-year-old. Kamala remains the same. Time has aged her, but not her mental strength or her deep belief in God. She guided me and remained strongly by my side through so many twists and turns in my life. Whenever I felt I was at a crossroad, Kamala would help me make the right choice. She is the woman behind all my successes and achievements.

She now dabbles a lot in philanthropy and enjoys her involvement much. We help people in need and donate to hospitals and organisations helping talented students without the financial ability to pursue their careers. God has given us enough. We both believe we should give it back to society, at least some of what it gave to us. Why should we stack our wealth? Nobody takes anything along when their journey is done. We lived a contented, happy life, and now our prayer is that we should enjoy the rest of it peacefully and get immersed in whatever good we can do unto others.

Author's son, daughter-in-law and grandsons

Epilogue

"True ethics begin where the use of language ceases."

– Albert Schweitzer

I would like to end just how I began—with another strand of wisdom taken from Ramakrishna Paramahansa. "He who has faith has all," the scholar F. Max Muller has quoted the saint as having said. Dwell on the thought for a while, and you will realise that in that small and simple sentence lies a deep profundity. Have faith, and the rest will follow. To me, that does not merely or only denote religious or spiritual faith; it means a fuller faith, faith as a system of values and ethics.

I would like to pass on some of what I learned over the past forty-two years of my professional career to others. I would like to dedicate this chapter to young leaders aspiring to climb the corporate ladder, hoping to lead the way someday in future. Success does not ooze from theories one learns in business schools; I never went to any. It comes from sustained honesty of purpose and determination, from remaining focused on tasks and accomplishing them. That is the core of my life experience. I would earnestly hope that these lessons will help budding young professionals transform into true leaders.

1. It is often debated whether a person is born with the qualities of a true leader or whether leadership skills can be acquired. I believe in the latter. One can consciously change one's behaviour and learn to shape oneself as a leader. Many qualities can be picked up during childhood, such as honesty, perseverance, respect for others and so on.

2. You should be uncompromising in the pursuit of excellence. I believe that this is the one goal I have singularly pursued all my life.

3. The goals and targets you decide must be high enough, in fact, a little beyond reach, a little beyond the limits of belief. Aim for the skies, and you will at least end up on the treetop. Build your convictions and back them up with hard work. Never accept underperformance, not least in yourself. Stay away from doubting Thomases; ruthlessly weed them out.

4. Never compromise on integrity. It is the fundamental quality of a leader.

5. A leader must be fair to all. The moment you are not, you lose respect.

6. The most important asset of any organisation is people. As you grow in the organisation, your people management skills must improve. At the level of a CEO, seventy per cent or more time is used to manage people. Unless you respect others, you cannot expect others to respect you. Relationships cannot be mechanical. Empathy towards people must come from within. You must understand and feel their moments of hope and despair.

7. You should provide honest feedback to people about their strengths and weaknesses. If you do not clearly communicate the weaknesses, you do harm by keeping them in a make-believe world. On the contrary, honest feedback works like magic.

8. While communicating difficult news, you must be straightforward, avoid long preambles, and get to the point. You should be able to clearly explain why a certain decision is being taken. It is painful but honest. It works best.

9. You must convey optimism. That doesn't mean you lie or mislead colleagues. If times are tough, spell that out and state what needs to be done in order to tide over adverse circumstances. Even as a team leader, if you are stressed, you should avoid passing it on to your team. Absorbing stress is part of what leadership should be. Besides, pessimism spreads quickly and destroys morale.

10. Innovation should be the heart and soul of any successful organisation. The spirit of innovation must percolate through the hierarchy. Every person must innovate in his/her own way without the fear of failing.

11. The CEO and top management must convey the sense that people should not be risk-averse for fear of failure and that failure should not be considered as underperformance and should not be punished. That doesn't mean you are creating an environment of failure. The effort to achieve the best results should be consistent and honest.

12. A leader must know the nitty-gritty of business and get his/her hands dirty. Many times, the leader needs to work shoulder-to-shoulder with the team. I never believed in micro-management; working with your team earns you respect and yields the best results.

13. You must remember that you are not indispensable. A true leader would prepare others to take over their role one day. Once you choose your successor, you should identify his/her strengths and weaknesses, communicate clearly, help and guide him/her to build on the strengths and cut out the weaknesses.

14. The goals you set must be conveyed clearly down the hierarchy. Often, it is found that people are working in different directions and are not aligned with the goals.

15. You must lie low and grounded. The limelight is always focused on the CEO. I have kept a low profile throughout my professional career. The moment you are swayed away by praise showered on you and start believing that you are the doyen of the industry and the most powerful person in the organisation, it is the end of your journey as a leader.

Acknowledgements

The list would be very long if I mentioned the names I owe my thanks for conceptualisation to publishing of this book. I am choosing a few among them without whose help this book couldn't have been written and published:

ABP Pvt. Ltd. for the photographs in pages 36 to 43, 48 to 51, 67, 68, 107 and 114.

Sankarshan Thakur, Editor, The Telegraph for editing the first manuscript and planning the flow of the book.

R. Rajagopal , Editor-At-Large, The Telegraph and his team for copy editing the manuscript.

Saktidas Roy, Chief Librarian, ABP Pvt. Ltd. for his help in pulling out the photographs from archive.

Subhendu Chaki, Senior Photographer, ABP Pvt. Ltd. for the Cover Photograph of the Author.

Amitava Chandra, Design Direrctor, ABP Pvt. Ltd. for design and Manoj Vasant Mahamunkar, Chief Manager Scanning & Colour Processing, Ananda Offset Pvt. Ltd. for colour correction of the Cover photograph.

Oommen Thomas, National Head, Ad sales, ABP Pvt. Ltd. for the photograph in page 116.

Ritesh Chakraborty for the photograph in page 119.

Suman Banerjee, CHRO, ABP Pvt. Ltd. for collection and placements of the photographs.

And finally, Yash Mehta, CEO, Education Business, Ananda Publishes Pvt. Ltd. for guidance, inspiration and help in publishing the book.

www.ingramcontent.com/pod-product-compliance
Lightning Source LLC
Chambersburg PA
CBHW032020140726
47988CB00017BA/675